SERRA DO

Iguaçu Falls

Uruguay

BRAZIL

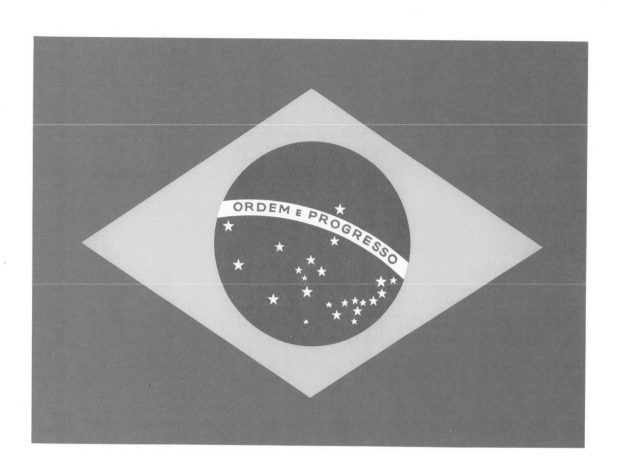

BRAZIL

By the Editors of Time-Life Books

TIME-LIFE BOOKS · ALEXANDRIA, VIRGINIA

TIME LIFE BOOKS ®

Other Publications:

THE TIME-LIFE GARDENER'S GUIDE
MYSTERIES OF THE UNKNOWN
TIME FRAME
FIX IT YOURSELF
FITNESS, HEALTH & NUTRITION
SUCCESSFUL PARENTING
HEALTHY HOME COOKING
UNDERSTANDING COMPUTERS
THE ENCHANTED WORLD
THE KODAK LIBRARY OF
   CREATIVE PHOTOGRAPHY
GREAT MEALS IN MINUTES
THE CIVIL WAR
PLANET EARTH
COLLECTOR'S LIBRARY OF THE CIVIL WAR
THE EPIC OF FLIGHT
THE GOOD COOK
WORLD WAR II
HOME REPAIR AND IMPROVEMENT
THE OLD WEST

This volume is one in a series of books
describing countries of the world—their
natural resources, peoples, histories,
economies and governments.

For information on and a full description of
any of the Time-Life Books series listed above,
please call 1-800-621-7026 or write:
Reader Information
Time-Life Customer Service
P.O. Box C-32068
Richmond, Virginia 23261-2068

Time-Life Books Inc.
is a wholly owned subsidiary of

TIME INCORPORATED

FOUNDER: HENRY R. LUCE 1898-1967

Editor-in-Chief: Henry Anatole Grunwald
Chairman and Chief Executive Officer: J. Richard Munro
President and Chief Operating Officer: N. J. Nicholas Jr.
Chairman of the Executive Committee: Ralph P. Davidson
Corporate Editor: Ray Cave
Executive Vice President, Books: Kelso F. Sutton
Vice President, Books: George Artandi

TIME-LIFE BOOKS INC.

EUROPEAN EDITOR: Kit van Tulleken
Assistant European Editor: Gillian Moore
Design Director: Ed Skyner
Photography Director: Pamela Marke
Chief of Research: Vanessa Kramer
Chief Sub-editor: Ilse Gray

LIBRARY OF NATIONS

Series Editor: Ellen Galford

Editorial Staff for *Brazil*
Editor: Martin Leighton
Researcher: Lesley Coleman
Designer: Lynne Brown
Sub-editor: Frances Dixon
Picture Department: Christine Hinze, Peggy Tout
Editorial Assistant: Molly Oates

EDITORIAL PRODUCTION

Production Assistants: Nikki Allen, Maureen Kelly
Editorial Department: Theresa John, Debra Lelliott

Contributors: The chapter texts were written by
Douglas Botting, Richard Bourne, Sue Branford,
Frederic V. Grunfeld and Patrick Knight.

Assistant Editor for the U.S. edition: Barbara Fairchild
Quarmby

CONSULTANTS

Robert Harvey is a regular contributor to
The Economist, London, and a member of
the British House of Commons; Isabel
Hilton is Latin-American correspondent
of *The Sunday Times,* London.

Second printing. Revised 1988.

Printed in U.S.A.
Published simultaneously in Canada.
School and library distribution by Silver Burdett
Company, Morristown, New Jersey.

TIME-LIFE is a trademark of Time Incorporated
U.S.A.

Library of Congress Cataloguing in Publication Data
Brazil
   (Library of nations)
   Bibliography: p.
   Includes index.
   1. Brazil.   I. Time-Life Books.   II. Series:
Library of Nations (Alexandria, Va.)
F2508.B847   1987   981   87-10125
ISBN 0-8094-5168-9
ISBN 0-8094-5169-7 (lib. bdg.)

Cover: Silhouetted against a threatening sky,
the 125-foot statue of Christ the Redeemer
dominates the city of Rio de Janeiro from the
2,310-foot summit of Corcovado (Hunchback)
Mountain.

Pages 1 and 2: The emblem on page 1,
which includes the date that the Brazilian
empire became a republic, is surrounded
by branches of coffee and tobacco plants. The
green background of the national flag on page
2 symbolizes the agricultural wealth of the
country, and the golden diamond shape its
huge mineral resources. In the center of the
flag, the motto "Order and Progress" is set
against a map of the constellations as they
appear over Rio de Janeiro.

Front and back endpapers: A topographic map
showing the major rivers, mountain ranges
and other natural features of Brazil appears
on the front endpaper; the back endpaper
shows the country's 26 states and territories,
and the principal towns.

CONTENTS

1 16
South America's Striving Giant
34 Picture Essay: The Beach as a Way of Life

2 42
Quests and Conquests

3 62
Rich and Poor, Black and White
78 Picture Essay: Cowboys of the Pampas

4 86
An Economic Roller Coaster
104 Picture Essay: Building Itaipu: A Colossus among Dams

5 112
A Cultural Melting Pot
128 Picture Essay: Land of Many Gods

6 136
Opening Up the Last Frontier

156 **Acknowledgments**
156 **Picture Credits**
156 **Bibliography**
158 **Index**

Nestling between the mountains and the sea, Rio de Janeiro justifies its reputation as one of the most beautiful cities in the world. The white sweep of

the famed Copacabana Beach *(center)*, fringed by hotels and apartment buildings, connects with downtown Rio *(right)* through a series of tunnels.

THE VANISHING GUARDIANS OF THE GRASSLANDS

Like the cowboys of the North American West, the gauchos of Brazil once tended herds of cattle that ranged freely over the pampas of the southern states. Now, although the grasslands are fenced in and jeeps have become a common mode of transportation, the gauchos still maintain a proud tradition of horsemanship and cultivate a spirit of self-reliance that is very similar to that of the cowboys of Hollywood mythology.

The gauchos are, however, part of a diminishing breed since Brazil, in only 40 years, has switched from being a predominantly agricultural to an industrial society, a turnabout that has gone hand in hand with the country's rapid urbanization. Of the economically active population, 68 percent were engaged in agriculture in 1940; only 13 percent worked in manufacturing and mining. By 1980, only 30 percent were in agriculture, while the percentage of those in manufacturing, mining and construction had doubled. In the same period those in service industries grew from 19 percent to 46 percent *(chart, below)*.

In addition to the shift into manufacturing and service industries, the number of agricultural workers is declining as a result of modern farming methods. Many ranchers have introduced foreign breeds of cattle and increasingly feed them scientifically rather than by natural pasturage.

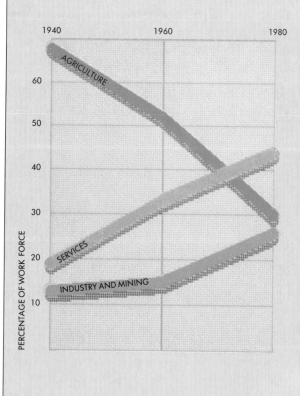

Wearing the accouterments of his calling, a gaucho from Rio Grande do Sul proudly sits his horse. His traditional *bombachas*, baggy trousers, are

8

tucked into soft leather boots that have circular spurs; a white scarf, sometimes used to shoo unruly cattle, is tied to his right wrist.

RIO'S EXTRAVAGANZA

Carnival—for many Catholics, a final fling before Lent—is celebrated throughout Brazil with spectacular parades, music and dancing in which the samba has become an essential element. No Carnival, however, compares with that of Rio de Janeiro, whose untrammeled high spirits and extravagance have made it Brazil's biggest tourist attraction.

Rio's festival culminates in an 80,000-strong parade of Carnival societies, called samba schools, competing for the title of Champion of the Avenue. Some schools spend up to $500,000 a year on the costumes for troupes that may number 3,000 members. To raise funds, some have turned into big business ventures that put on year-round performances in Brazil and abroad, sell records and publish magazines.

More than one third of the 1.7 million annual visitors to Brazil come for the Rio Carnival. But a growing number of foreign tourists are drawn by the spectacular natural attractions, such as the Iguaçu Falls in the south, the seemingly endless tropical beaches of Brazil's Atlantic seaboard, and the mysterious Amazon River, best seen from the city of Manaus.

In the nine-hour parade that climaxes Rio's Carnival, a samba school gyrates down the Sambódromo, a .4-mile-long avenue in the city center flanked

by permanent reviewing stands and boxes. The schools are divided into three leagues and are judged on dancing as well as on costumes and floats.

A YOUTHFUL POPULATION

Brazil is a young nation not only in historical terms but demographically. With more than 132 million inhabitants, the country has one of the world's fastest-growing populations: half of it less than 20 years old, and 65 percent under 30. The birth rate, however, is much higher in rural areas, where households average six children, compared with three in urban families. One consequence is that the infant mortality rate varies considerably: In the poor, sparsely populated northeastern states it is as high as 140 per 1,000, against 54 per 1,000 in the urbanized south.

The occupants of a single house in the town of Juázeiro do Norte, in the northeastern state of Ceará, gather on their front stoop. Such extended

families are typical in this arid region, where the men earn their living as subsistence farmers or as peons on sugar plantations.

A newly constructed road cuts through primeval rain forest near Jari, north of the Amazon River. Hastily built during the 1970s and for the most part

14

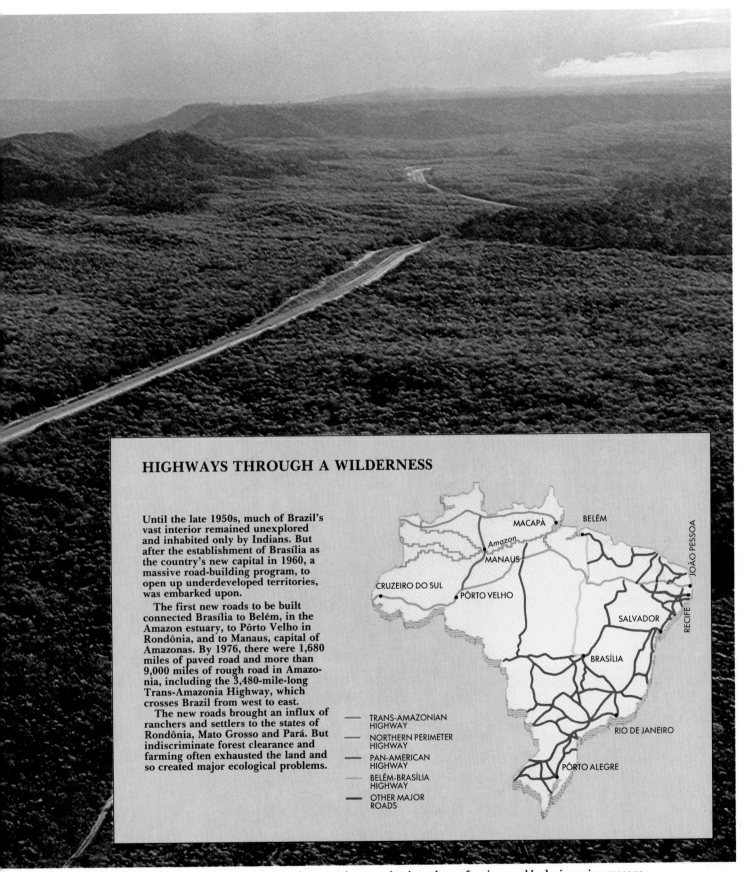

HIGHWAYS THROUGH A WILDERNESS

Until the late 1950s, much of Brazil's vast interior remained unexplored and inhabited only by Indians. But after the establishment of Brasília as the country's new capital in 1960, a massive road-building program, to open up underdeveloped territories, was embarked upon.

The first new roads to be built connected Brasília to Belém, in the Amazon estuary, to Pôrto Velho in Rondônia, and to Manaus, capital of Amazonas. By 1976, there were 1,680 miles of paved road and more than 9,000 miles of rough road in Amazonia, including the 3,480-mile-long Trans-Amazonia Highway, which crosses Brazil from west to east.

The new roads brought an influx of ranchers and settlers to the states of Rondônia, Mato Grosso and Pará. But indiscriminate forest clearance and farming often exhausted the land and so created major ecological problems.

TRANS-AMAZONIAN HIGHWAY
NORTHERN PERIMETER HIGHWAY
PAN-AMERICAN HIGHWAY
BELÉM-BRASÍLIA HIGHWAY
OTHER MAJOR ROADS

unpaved, many highways in Amazonia have proved extremely expensive to maintain and are often impassable during rainy seasons.

Twin skyscrapers housing parliamentary offices soar above the main square of Brasília, the capital of Brazil. The young city, completed in 1960, stands at the center of a new transportation and communications network that has opened up the vast Brazilian wilderness.

SOUTH AMERICA'S STRIVING GIANT

For more than a century and a half, Brazilians talked about building a capital city in the heart of their vast country. The reasons were compelling. Rio de Janeiro, the capital since 1763, was a seaport whose cultural and economic horizons were focused on the lands across the Atlantic Ocean, to the neglect of its hinterland—a territory 15 times larger than France. Between the late 18th century and the middle of the 20th, various proposals for a new capital were made, but it was not until 1955 that a location was finally selected. The site that was chosen was an area of nearly 2,400 square miles of semiarid scrubland 3,300 feet up on the Goiás plateau, more than four hours by road from the nearest sizable town and more than 600 miles from Rio de Janeiro.

Even then the project might have foundered but for the dynamism of the republic's newly elected president, Juscelino Kubitschek, who was convinced that the transfer of the capital from the coast was essential if Brazil was to look to the interior and develop its wealth of agricultural and mineral resources. In September of 1956, Kubitschek signed a state order establishing an umbrella construction body, Novacap (short for New Capital); he thus set in motion the most ambitious city-building project of the 20th century.

A plan for the new capital, which was to be called Brasília, had been chosen in a competition open to the country's architects. Drawn by Lúcio Costa, the winning proposal set the city along two main axes, crossing at right angles, one of them curved like the wing of an airplane. Oscar Niemeyer, the internationally famous architect whose work includes the United Nations Building in New York City, was commissioned to design the principal buildings. Massive loans were obtained to finance the project: All that was needed were the raw materials and a labor force able to work to a crippling schedule, for President Kubitschek had named the 21st of August, 1960, as the inauguration date for the new capital.

The Novacap project recruited its labor force from a massive influx of migrants from the drought-ridden northeast, and to house them, it built an encampment 16 miles outside the city. Called Free City because it was exempt from taxes, it grew into a wild, sprawling town that looked like a Hollywood set for a Western, with wooden-fronted buildings and false second stories, unpaved streets and rickety board sidewalks—all coated in the ubiquitous red dust of the region. Jeeps rather than horses were parked in front of the 101 bars, 30 hotels and 35 boarding houses in Free City, and these offered accommodations and entertainment at astronomically high prices.

For most of the town's 45,000 inhabitants there was little time to relax. They often worked as many as 15 hours a day, sometimes grabbing a nap while a draftsman hastily put the finishing

1

In the northeastern state of Ceará, where the annual rainfall averages only 20 to 25 inches, a landscape of scrub and stone bakes under a cloudless sky. Most of the inhabitants of the area, which is the hottest and driest of Brazil, earn a subsistence living as cattle farmers.

touches on a design for a building already nearing completion. Thanks to these indefatigable *candangos,* as the immigrants from the northeast are called, Kubitschek was able to keep to his timetable. On the designated day, after fewer than four years of construction, the new capital was formally inaugurated. No one seemed to mind that most of the hotels and apartment buildings were still unfurnished; that the foreign newspaper correspondents slept on straw mattresses on the floors of windowless houses; and that the inaugural Mass was held in an unfinished cathedral. Brasília was launched with great fanfare and fireworks—not only was it the first entirely modern city in the world, but it was the capital of a far-flung nation giving notice to the rest of the world that it was assuming its place in the 20th century and staking a claim to the 21st.

As might be expected, many Brazilians were opposed to the grandiose scheme. Back in Rio de Janeiro, Senate debates about financial scandals involving Novacap turned into brawls. Any estimate of the final cost involved would be a guess, but by the time the new capital was inaugurated, expenditure on it had exceeded the total amount of currency that had been in circulation in Brazil when Kubitschek took office; the country's foreign debt was so out of hand that Brazil was already in trouble with the International Monetary Fund; and domestic inflation had soared as well.

Many government employees were unhappy about moving away from Rio; some of them were concerned that their property investments would suffer once the city ceased to be the capital, and all of them were dismayed at the prospect of living in a city so far from

the sea, for coastal Brazilians tend to judge a city by the number and quality of its beaches. Kubitschek enticed the doubters by offering a 100 percent salary increase to civil servants prepared to work in Brasília. It took longer to persuade foreign embassies and some state corporations to leave the commercial centers of Rio and São Paulo, but by 1974, all government business was being conducted from the new capital.

Today, Brasília has a population of more than one million, living in eight satellite towns. Some of the earliest buildings are cracking, but the capital

A superimposed map shows that Brazil, occupying 3,286,488 square miles, could easily swallow Europe from the Irish coast to the East German border. However, only about 40 people inhabit each square mile of the world's fifth-largest country, which covers nearly half of South America.

still has the appearance of a showpiece of the space age—an architectural model of itself—with acres of glass reflecting the futuristic wedges and curves of architect Niemeyer's buildings, which are laid out on broad avenues crossed by spectacular underpasses and overpasses.

It is not a pedestrian's city. Only cars move on the streets, giving the city a strangely deserted, sometimes sinister, look—a "terrifying preview of a collectivist future," commented American historian Arthur Schlesinger. Nor is it a city for the proletariat. Although a

1

A roughly paved street climbs through the hill town of Horto in the northeast of Brazil. Although the houses are small and simple, the town is more prosperous than others in the region because sugar cane is grown in the area, providing work for many of the people who live there.

grateful government erected a monument in the center of the city to the *candangos* who had built Brasília, those same workers were relentlessly expelled and set up their own *favelas,* or shantytowns, outside the city limits. Many of these *favelas* stand cheek by jowl with affluent suburbs of red-tiled houses set beside green lawns and blue swimming pools.

Yet even with its *favelas* and glaring inequalities of wealth, Brasília stands as the most spectacular symbol of Brazil's transformation from a quasi-colonial agricultural economy into a modern, 20th-century industrial state. It is a

country that has been called a land of never-ending impossibilities—a land that has the eighth-largest economy in the Western world and that has a larger foreign debt than any other country; a land where an executive may earn 200 times more than a worker but where the 30,000 richest people pay an average of 1.3 percent of their incomes in taxes; a land with one of the most rapidly growing populations in the world, but with half its territory no more densely populated than the Sahara. How these contradictions will be resolved is unclear. Brazil is poised, like an imago newly emerged from its

chrysalis, drying its wings and still vulnerable, on the threshold of an unpredictable political and economic future.

This transformation is taking place against the backdrop of an enormous physical geography. With an area of 3,286,488 square miles, Brazil takes up 47 percent of the South American continent and is the fifth-largest country in the world, after the U.S.S.R., Canada, China and the United States. Moreover, it has more potentially useful territory than any other country in the world, since it has neither inaccessible mountains, burning deserts nor frozen

Wheat fields stretch to the horizon in the fertile state of Paraná, which is named after the parasol-shaped Paraná pine, such as the one towering above the farmhouse. Enjoying the temperate climate of southeastern Brazil, Paraná is a major producer of grain, cotton, coffee and legumes.

wastes. About three eighths of this territory lies in the basin of the Amazon, which from its source in the Andes roughly follows the line of the equator to the Atlantic, close to the spot where the Portuguese navigator Pedro Álvares Cabral claimed Brazil for his country in 1500. The rest of the country is basically a huge plateau, rising to a maximum elevation of almost 10,000 feet, but with an average altitude of only 1,640 feet.

What Brazil lacks in extremes of relief, it makes up for in the scale of its natural features. Its coastline measures more than 4,300 miles and could al-most have been created by nature as a playground for the ubiquitous Brazilian cult of the body beautiful, since it provides all the great port cities of Belém, Recife, Rio de Janeiro, Salvador and Santos with magnificent beaches at which to swim, surf or simply sunbathe.

Connecting the interior to the sea are extensive river systems, of which the longest completely within Brazil is the São Francisco, which loops for 1,988 miles through the arid northeastern heartland to the temperate southeast. It is known as the "river of national unity" because it brings together the four corners of Brazil. In the south, the rivers that form the River Plate system—the Paraguay, Uruguay and Paraná, the third-longest river of the Americas—partly flow through Brazil.

But it is the mighty Amazon that seizes the imagination—the greatest river in the world, rivaling the Nile in length and carrying at least 50 times its volume, flowing for 4,000 miles through the world's largest rain forest. Brazil's timber reserves are the world's third largest, after the Soviet Union's and Canada's, three quarters of which are found in Amazonia, whose forests—spread like a vast green *bouclé* carpet over more than one million square miles—boast 400 species of hardwood alone. Among them are jacarandas, mahogany and the brazilwood tree, which the first Portuguese colonists exploited for its dye, and which has given its name to the country.

Brazil's other natural resources include immense mineral wealth. It is the world's largest source of aquamarine, topaz, bauxite and niobium. Brazil has gold reserves of 33,000 tons and iron-ore deposits estimated at 33 billion tons of almost 66 percent pure iron; it has the world's fourth-largest deposits of manganese and the fifth-largest reserves of uranium. Enough oil has been found offshore to supply all the country's needs by the 1990s. Agriculture, the original basis of Brazil's wealth, is still an important source of export earnings, employing 30 percent of the total work force and earning nearly 40 percent of export income. Brazil is the world's largest producer and exporter of coffee and sugar cane, the second largest of cocoa; it also exports soybeans, tobacco and fruit. And in the 1980s, Brazil overtook the United States as the world's leading exporter of orange juice.

But Brazil's most vital resource is its people. With more than 132 million, of which nearly 65 percent are under the age of 30, it is the sixth most populous nation on earth, and one of the fastest growing, having doubled its population between 1960 and 1985. There is no such thing as a "typical" Brazilian, because virtually every part of the world has contributed at least some share to the genetic pool. A Brazilian might be descended from European settlers, indigenous Amerindians, African blacks, Asian immigrants—or any combination of these.

Although Brazilians are proud of

their reputation as a melting-pot society in which there is a high degree of racial tolerance, most of them recognize four "color" groups in the population: whites, mainly of European ancestry, who form nearly 62 percent of the population; browns, mostly of mixed-blood descent, who constitute 27 percent of Brazilians; blacks, the descendants of African slaves, who account for 11 percent of the total; and yellows, almost entirely the descendants of Japanese immigrants, who make up less than 1 percent.

In fact, intermarriage has been such a feature of Brazilian society that these distinctions are too blurred to have much significance. They reflect social and economic status rather than racial origins. By and large, the whiter a Brazilian's skin, the greater his opportunities and the higher his social standing; "whiteness" is determined as much by a person's job, clothes, education and manner as by skin color, so that a wealthy, well-educated businessperson will be regarded as a "white" regardless of his or her skin color. Ironically, the one group that has been—and to an extent, still is—victimized by racial prejudice represents the purest strain in Brazilian society: the 200,000 or so Indians of the rain forests.

Despite the size of the population, Brazil is one of the more sparsely settled parts of the globe, with an average of 40 people per square mile—compared with an average of 65 people per square mile in the United States, which has slightly more land area. Moreover, the population is very unevenly distributed, with more than 90 percent of it concentrated in the coastal states and only 4 percent scattered through the Amazon basin, which occupies nearly

Skyscrapers dwarf pink-blossomed shrubs in central São Paulo *(left)*, Brazil's largest city and the hub of the country's economy. Although it had only 31,000 inhabitants a century ago, today the city teems with more than 11 million people, of richly diverse ethnic origins *(above)*.

1

half the country. Even more striking are the contrasts in living standards between the people in different parts of the country. In the industrialized south, for example, the level of personal income is three times higher than it is in the northeast, where almost one seventh of the population has neither permanent work nor land. In a city such as Brasília, more than 90 percent of households have electricity and municipal water; in rural regions of the north, 90 percent or more do not.

Disparities like these fall into a marked regional pattern, recognized by the Brazilian authorities themselves. The authorities have assigned the country's 23 federal states and three territories to five much larger regions, each of which embraces areas that roughly share economic or agricultural problems. Others distinguish six regions: the northeast coast; the arid northeast *sertão,* or back country; the industrialized southeast, centered on Rio and São Paulo; the mixed farming region of the south; the central west; and the north, which includes most of the Amazon basin.

Each of these six regions is distinguished not only by climate and topography, but also by the historical patterns of settlement and economic development based on some primary product—sugar on the northeast coast, coffee and gold in the southeast, rubber in the Amazon. Furthermore, each region has evolved in comparative isolation, having had virtually no contact with its neighbors, which lends support to the view that "Brazil is a continent with its colonies inside it."

The oldest of these colonies is the fertile strip of the northeast coast, a "great, wild, untidy, luxuriant hothouse" ac-cording to naturalist Charles Darwin, who visited the region in the 1830s. The colony's first export was brazilwood, which was traded from the settlements around Recife, but by the middle of the 16th century, the timber trade had been eclipsed by the lucrative sugar industry. For a century, northeastern Brazil enjoyed a virtual world monopoly of the industry, which was centered on Salvador, the country's first capital. Even today, the splendid and numerous 17th-century churches and public buildings attest to the former wealth of the colony, and Salvador, which is usually referred to as Bahia, the name of the state of which it is the capital, has become an important cultural center with a thriving colony of artists and writers who believe Salvador to be the country's most quintessentially Brazilian city. The sugar industry still plays an important role in the local and national economy, for in addition to traditional food products, cane sugar provides the alcohol that now helps to power more than 40 percent of the country's motor vehicles.

The northeast coast is also the region where the cultures of Europe and Africa first came together. Music, dance, religion, language, literature—the whole social and cultural fabric of the nation—have been decisively influenced by the approximately five million black slaves who were shipped from Africa to work on the sugar plantations. Although Brazil was the last Western country to abolish slavery—in 1888—there were few taboos on mixed marriages, and many of the plantation owners took black mistresses. The resulting infusion of African culture is very palpable today in the towns and cities of the northeast, where dark faces predominate, where women dress in West African-style swathes of brightly colored cloth and where the samba, derived from African rhythms, blares from loudspeakers in the street. According to the distinguished writer Jorge Amado, Africa's contribution to the Brazilian character was crucial. "The black man," he says, "has saved us from melancholy and sadness."

On the plateau above the northeastern coastal strip, the harsh face of tropical Brazil is manifest. This is the northeastern *sertão,* or back country—"one of the poorest places on earth" according to the British journalist James Cameron, who added that it was "known as the land of *miseria morte:* the sorrows of death." The *sertão* was first settled as a cattle-raising region, supplying the coastal sugar plantations, but it has never prospered. It is a giant dust bowl—almost 350,000 square miles of arid savanna, scrub forest, cactus and thorn bushes—that has been stricken by cycles of drought every eight to 15 years, and then devastated by floods. In 1984, for example, a five-year drought ended in torrential rainstorms that left 150 people dead or missing and 700,000 people homeless.

Of the 35 million people who live in the region, the most distinctive are the *vaqueiros*—the northeastern version of the Brazilian cowboy—who drive their scrawny cattle huge distances in search of pasture. Other inhabitants of the region practice subsistence farming or collect wild gums and waxes that are used in paint and varnish manufacture. But many people have to migrate to earn a living, spending two or three years working on major civil engineering projects all over the country or finding jobs as construction workers in the burgeoning cities of the southeast, where they often live in the buildings

24

they are erecting. Yet they tend to be fiercely loyal to their harsh land, and most return when they have saved enough money or hear that the rains are falling again at home.

While all but a handful of sugar plantation owners in the northeast have never known wealth, the outward signs of prosperity are very apparent 600 miles farther south, in the huge modern cities of Rio de Janeiro and São Paulo. Their wealth was founded on gold discovered in the hills of the eastern highlands, almost 200 miles inland from the coast. The precious metal was discovered at the end of the 17th century and so set off Brazil's second boom, attracting hundreds of thousands of prospectors to Ouro Prêto, meaning "Black Gold," a town that derived its name from the fact that the gold found in its mines turned black on exposure to the air, owing to the presence of silver in the lode. The state in which most of the discoveries were made was named simply Minas Gerais, or "General Mines."

During much of the 18th century, the mines of Minas Gerais provided nearly half of the world's annual output of gold, in addition to a total of three million carats of diamonds. With their new-found wealth, the gold miners and

1

merchants turned Ouro Prêto into the finest city in the colony. At the height of its prosperity, the city had a population of 100,000, splendid baroque churches, graceful public squares and fountains, and elegant private homes decorated with statuary. Sometimes, though, the new rich of Minas Gerais spent their money on extravagances: One man, for example, built an artifical lake on which he launched a sailing ship so that his mulatto female slave, who had never traveled by sea, could savor the experience.

By the beginning of the 19th century, however, the gold deposits were nearly exhausted, and by 1821, an English traveler reported that Ouro Prêto "scarcely retains a shadow of its former splendor." Today, with a population of approximately 25,000, Ouro Prêto is a national monument—a major tourist attraction for Brazilians who come to admire their baroque heritage and to examine the square where Brazil's first revolutionary martyr, Joaquim José da Silva Xavier, is commemorated. Known as Tiradentes, the "Toothpuller," because he was a part-time dentist, Xavier was hanged and quartered in Rio de Janeiro in 1789 for leading a conspiracy against Portuguese colonial rule.

Minas Gerais is still endowed with a great store of mineral wealth, including a mountain so rich in iron that cars and trucks crossing it have to shift into low gear and accelerate in order to overcome the magnetic force that impedes their progress. Some of the local ore is processed at Belo Horizonte, the capital of Minas Gerais since 1897, and now a city with a population of two million, producing wagons, tractors, cement, textiles, shoes and foodstuffs.

One of the few towns in the southeast that weathered the collapse of the gold

boom was Rio de Janeiro. Established as the gateway to the mining regions, it soon assumed such importance that, in 1763, it replaced Salvador as the capital, doubling in size to 120,000 inhabitants over the next 10 years. When the gold mines had been exhausted, Rio was perfectly positioned to take advantage of the country's next great economic boom—coffee. The hilly, fertile land lying behind the capital was ideal for cultivating the coffee shrub, which takes only three to five years to reach maturity and continues to produce abundantly for more than 30 years. By 1810, coffee plantations were spread throughout the state of Rio de Janeiro as well as Minas Gerais; by 1830, Brazil was producing more than 40 percent of the world's supply; and by 1870, coffee had become the country's most important product.

One suspects, however, that Rio would have survived and prospered even without coffee. The city "has edged in between the hills and the sea," wrote the English traveler Peter Fleming, "and on that boldly chosen strip of land has met and trounced the jungle. She gleams up at you complacently, a successful opportunist."

Rio de Janeiro qualifies as one of the two or three most beautiful cities in the world, with a natural setting surpassing even Hong Kong's and San Francisco's. Nestling between blue-green mountains and the turquoise sea, the city stretches for more than 12 miles along a magnificent bay whose 16 beaches are interrupted here and there by huge domes of rock that have been worn to pebble roundness by the passage of geological time.

Visitors accustomed to less theatrical cityscapes may find an air of unreality

At the Iguaçu Falls, where Brazil, Argentina and Paraguay meet, more than 450,000 cubic feet of water per second pour over the precipice during the flood months. Visiting First Lady Eleanor Roosevelt said this cluster of 275 cataracts made Niagara Falls look like a kitchen faucet.

about Rio. "The hand of nature (powerfully aided by the hand of man) stuns new arrivals into a sort of happy dream where anything may happen," wrote Philip Guedalla, an English writer. "Suburban streets end suddenly against the gray flank of a lonely mountain that has somehow got forgotten in a residential neighborhood; roads climb out of a shopping district into the dripping silence of a forest in the tropics, where the big lianas hang and unimagined flowers blaze in the shadow of the trees, and drivers of oncoming traffic are apt to be bewildered by enormous blue butterflies flapping slowly toward them; and a road tunnel full of trams opens incredibly upon the sudden blue of unexpected bays that curve between a line of big Atlantic rollers and a tall plantation where the palms are full of enthusiasts watching American football."

Rio's theatrical air is overwhelming during the Carnival celebrations—the annual public madness that goes on continuously from the preceding Friday to the morning of Ash Wednesday. Originally a Catholic religious festival, Carnival has been transformed by a vigorous infusion of African energy into an activity symbolic of everything the world regards as quintessentially Brazilian—beautiful women, dashing men, outrageous costumes and sexual high jinks; the whole thing moving to the rhythm of the samba.

To the thousands of foreign tourists who visit Rio each year, the less appealing aspects of the city are not readily apparent. They do not have to contend every day with the monumental traffic jams, the consequence of its mountain-choked topography and population of five million. To visitors moving between the beaches and the elegant shopping complexes of the high-rise center, the pastel-colored *favelas* clustered on the mountainsides may seem picturesque, even romantic, especially during the preparations for Carnival, when the throb of practicing samba drummers mingles with the workaday sounds of the city.

In reality, the *favelas,* which house almost a quarter of Rio's population, are noisome slums, in which only a tiny proportion of households have running water, sewage facilities or electricity. In the absence of public medical facilities or unemployment benefits for the 30 to 40 percent out of work in the *favelas,* social problems multiply. For these inhabitants of Brazil's "Third World," the glittering "First World" spread out below them is a place experienced only during the frenetic days of Carnival, or through the television in the corner bar, or through crime. Every day there are between 400 and 500 personal robbery assaults in Rio, and visitors are constantly advised about the areas or streets or times of day in which it is unsafe to be abroad.

Year after year, the *favelas* continue to grow as landless peasants exchange the grinding poverty of the countryside for urban squalor. Indeed, one of the most striking phenomena of Brazil is the rapid growth of the cities, which has gone hand in hand with the rapid industrialization of the postwar years. In 1940, only 31 percent of the population lived in the cities, but by 1970, the figure had risen to 56 percent, and by 1980, two thirds of the population were city dwellers.

Brazil's fastest-growing city is São Paulo, 220 miles southwest of Rio. Although it was founded as early as 1554, its population was only 31,000 in the 1870s, when coffee planters began to move into the region. By 1885, the region had supplanted the state of Rio de Janeiro as the center of coffee production, and by 1920, São Paulo's population had risen to over half a million. Four years later, it overtook Rio as the most important industrial center in Latin America, although it was not until the 1960s that its population actually overtook Rio's. At the beginning of that decade the population of São Paulo was about 3.7 million. By the end of the decade, it was six million, and it has gone on growing at the rate of 350,000 a year. Today, the population of the greater metropolitan area stands at 15 million, making São Paulo the largest city in South America; its thoroughly urban atmosphere includes a skyscraper skyline reminiscent of Chicago.

Largely due to the availability of hydroelectric power in the south, about half of Brazil's industrial production comes from São Paulo. Another factor in the phenomenal growth of the city is its elevation of 2,700 feet above sea level, which gives it a pleasant temperate climate that has helped attract many skilled European immigrants, plus 200,000 Japanese. Brazilians such as these brag of their spirit and enterprise. They criticize the people of Rio as lazy and unambitious, and they complain of the social and economic drag of the other regions, citing the Brazilian saying that "Brazil is made up of one locomotive and 20 boxcars." São Paulo is, of course, the locomotive, and the other states are the boxcars.

Descendants of European immigrants, mainly from Germany and Italy, constitute more than half of the population of the south, which has a greater variety of topography, climate and vegetation than any other Brazilian region. Inland

features include the forest-clad valleys of the Paraná and Uruguay rivers, which mark the western boundary of the region; the low, rolling grasslands that extend into Rio Grande do Sul from Uruguay; and forested uplands that reach their highest point in Paraná. Unlike regions farther north, the south has never had a society divided between plantation owners and slaves, nor has it had an economic boom and bust. Instead, it has grown steadily in prosperity, its wealth based on mixed farming and pampas cattle ranching.

Many of the farmers who emigrated to the south clung to their European heritage, refusing to speak Portuguese and building their homes and barns in a style that reminded them of home. At the outbreak of World War II, at least 75 percent of the inhabitants of Blumenau, not far from the coastal city of Florianópolis, spoke German, and Nazi propaganda and pro-Axis sentiment were rife. The Brazilian government responded by prohibiting teaching in any language but Portuguese, and by sending German Brazilian youths to do their national service in the north, where they were forced to learn the national language, and where their views on racial purity were modified by contact with beautiful mulatto women. Nowadays, their descendants are more thoroughly assimilated, but the German language is still widely spoken and still, unofficially, used in schools. In Blumenau, rousing brass bands in Tyrolean hats play for the customers in the *Weinstuben,* which serve local wines.

On the prairie-like pampas in the far south, cattle ranching is the main economic activity. The cowboys in this area are called *gaúchos,* like their Argentine counterparts, and tend to look down on their poorer colleagues, the *vaqueiros* of the northeast. They still wear their traditional gaúcho hats, balloon-pleated trousers and brightly colored shirts; they drink hot maté tea out of a chimarrão gourd, and they are, of course, superb horsemen.

The *gaúchos* are a drawing card for tourists, but the region's main scenic attraction is the Iguaçu Falls, near the point where Brazil, Argentina and Paraguay come together. Plunging over a 230-foot-high precipice are the combined waters of some 30 rivers and streams from the interior of Paraná. During the three flood months beginning in May, the water falls at the rate of more than 459,088 cubic feet per second—almost as much as the Amazon River pours into the sea.

Brazil's fifth region, the central west, includes the states of Goiás and Mato Grosso, and the federal district of Brasília. The most uniform of the regions, it is part of the great Brazilian plateau, covered with dense tropical forests in the north and subtropical savanna and scrub elsewhere. In size and remoteness it is surpassed only by the Amazon basin to the north; it accounts for 22 percent of the national territory and has large tracts unexplored even today. But it is also Brazil's fastest growing region (although its population still represents less than 7 percent of the total), attracting immigrants from all over the country.

Many of these newcomers head for the developed areas around Brasília and Goiás, which are major mining areas, while others carve out a new life in the virgin bush. Some of these pioneers are gold or diamond prospectors, others small-scale farmers. There are also wealthy ranchers—although some of these are more interested in making a killing in real estate than in raising cattle. These people have created an active frontier territory, complete with cowboys and Indians, prospectors and land speculators, where conflicting interests—especially between homesteaders and ranchers—have ended in gun fights and considerable loss of life.

The north, consisting almost entirely of the Amazon basin, is Brazil's last frontier—a wilderness bigger than India, with a population in 1980 of 7.5 million, giving it a density of 3.4 people per square mile, compared with more than 133 people per square mile in the south. Near the Colombian and Venezuelan frontiers to the north, there are great stretches of grassy plains, and along the Venezuelan border, Brazil's highest mountains rise nearly 10,000 feet. But most of the region is densely forested lowland, veined with great rivers that provided the only highways until the 1960s. "The forest of the Amazons is not merely trees and shrubs," wrote British writer H. M. Tomlinson. "It is not land. It is another element. Its inhabitants are arborean; they have been fashioned for life in that medium as fishes to the sea and birds to the air. Its green apparition is persistent as the sky is and the ocean."

Contrary to appearances, the land is surprisingly infertile and the economy of the region has traditionally been geared to the collection of forest products—chiefly nuts, oils, fine woods, medicinal herbs and wild rubber. Most of Amazonia's small-scale farmers and gatherers live along the rivers in houses of thatch or planks built on banks or stilts so that they are above the seasonal flood level. Modern Brazil scarcely impinges on these people. Their Catholicism is strongly laced with Indian customs; illiteracy is more than 60 percent; and infant mortality is shockingly high. Contact with the outside world is maintained primarily through river traders, who periodically stop at the settlements to exchange the amenities of civilization for forest products. Many such communities live in virtual debt-bondage to these river traders, who are

Crossing the unpaved roadbed of the Trans-Amazonian Highway, poachers carry the body of a jaguar from the dense rain forest. Hunters who supply skins and furs to the high-fashion world often use light aircraft and automatic weapons in the pursuit of their illegal trade.

1

themselves often heavily in debt to their suppliers in the towns.

A large proportion of Amazonia's non-Indian population is descended from migrants from the northeast, who settled in the region during a rubber boom that began in the 1880s and lasted barely 30 years. The center of the market was Manaus, three to five days' journey upriver, which the rubber barons turned into a 19th-century metrop-olis to vie with Rio. But when the boom went bust the lights of Manaus went out, and the region lapsed into tropical torpor once more.

For 40 years, Amazonia remained a backwater, but in the 1960s, the Brazilian government, worried about the consequences of leaving half the country untenanted and undeveloped, took steps to bring the region into the economic and political mainstream. In 1965, they decided to turn Manaus into a free port, with generous tax incentives, and over the next 15 years the city's fortunes were revived. In the mid-1980s, it had a population of more than 650,000 inhabitants and boasted an important electronics industry.

In an effort to open up the region, the government financed the construction of the 3,480-mile-long Trans-Amazonian Highway, from João Pes-

In an experimental government project, fast-growing Caribbean pine saplings wait to be planted in a newly cleared Amazonian woodland. The goal of the experiment is to find a species suitable for wood-pulping that will thrive in the poor forest soils.

soa on the Atlantic seaboard right through the rain forest to Peru in the west, together with thousands of miles of other main roads. Throughout the 1970s, buses streamed down the new highways, carrying migrant farmers from the *sertão*, people, like their 19th-century predecessors, impelled by the dream of carving out a successful living in the forest. The large-scale settlement of Amazonia is a contentious issue however—partly because farms and ranches that replace trees often have to be abandoned within a few years, victims of the poor soil, and partly because of fears that this unique environment, with the greatest collection of plants and animals on earth, will be destroyed forever.

The miracle of Brazil is that, huge and variegated as it is, with a population whose lifestyles vary dramatically from extreme wealth to dismal poverty, it is a unified country. Even given the contrasting fortunes of its regions, Brazil is one of the few great nations untroubled by separatist factions or regional autonomy movements. Despite the glaring economic gap between town and country, and between slum dwellers and their wealthy urban neighbors, there is remarkably little enthusiasm for Communism or revolutionary socialism. Despite the widely different ethnic backgrounds of the population and the long years of division into a "slave" class and a "gentleman" class, there is a strong feeling among Brazilians of all racial origins that they form one people and one nation. Brazil, like the United States, is a paradox of oneness encompassing diversity.

To an extent, unity has been imposed on the nation by a remarkable uniformity in the administrative and political structure of the disparate regions of the country. Brazil is a federal republic with a constitution based on that of the United States. It grants many powers to the legislatures of its 23 states, which have the right to deal with all matters affecting provincial administration and finance. Much political debate revolves around the relative powers of the federal government and the state legislatures. Nevertheless, from the Amazon rain forest to the southern pampas, state and municipal governments conform to the same system of education, public health, finance and other services.

Under the constitution of 1969, the federal Congress is made up of a 69-member Senate and a 479-member Chamber of Deputies. The Senate is two-thirds directly elected and one-third indirectly elected, while the Chamber of Deputies is elected by universal franchise. This franchise, however, was limited by a literacy qualification that effectively disenfranchised 40 percent of the population. It was only in 1985 that the literacy requirement was abolished and Brazil became truly democratic.

Democratic government has been suspended several times by both direct and indirect intervention of the military authorities, who have always regarded themselves as guarantors of the Brazilian constitution. But, by the standards of other South American countries, the coups that toppled elected governments were relatively bloodless, and the military regimes that took over were comparatively unrepressive. In 1985, after 21 years of military rule, major constitutional reforms were promised, to meet a popular demand for direct participation at all levels of government and, possibly, a devolution of powers from the federal government to the states.

National unity, however, does not stem from political institutions alone, and the lack of friction between the elements is the result of a number of historical factors. The kings of Portugal, often because they did not have the resources and power to impose their will, ruled Brazil in a tolerant manner, allowing the colonists freedom to develop in their own fashion. Historically, as well, the Portuguese language and the Roman Catholic Church were crucial unifying factors. Portuguese Catholicism, never as exigent as the Church in Spanish South America, proved as malleable as the colonial power. From Brazil's early days, for example, it took a permissive view of the sexual morals of the Portuguese settlers toward African and Indian women, and so opened the door to the great mixture of races that has become the Brazilian nation. Equally, after an initial attempt to suppress the religions brought to Brazil by the African slaves, the Church came to tolerate them, and even absorbed African religious practices and gods into its own liturgy and family of saints.

This was a major consideration in a nation that claims to be the largest Roman Catholic community in the world, since it gave Brazil a cultural matrix that could be applied to all the various regions and peoples of the emerging nation. The new nation is certainly, as Jorge Amado says, "a hybrid nation, a hybrid people with a hybrid culture," but Brazil nevertheless has a unity that is unmistakable. It is that unity that makes him add: "What gives me confidence in Brazil is our capacity not to give in to poverty and oppression, but to fight and go forward." □

33

THE BEACH AS A WAY OF LIFE

With 4,600 miles of white sand strung out along the Atlantic seaboard and temperatures that rarely fall below 70°F., the beaches of Brazil are an irresistible magnet for anyone within reach of the coast. Pulsing with life, throbbing with samba music, the curving shores and palm-fringed inlets are meeting places for all races and classes. Bronzing in their scanty bikinis, young girls from the shantytowns lie down as equals beside heiresses from the glittering towers of Copacabana. Businessmen in bathing trunks stroll along, wheeling and dealing, as the ripples lap at their feet, barely noticing the volleyball players, the skin-divers, or the schoolchildren sprawled out doing their homework on the sand.

For some people, the beach is a marketplace, a bazaar of balloons, costume jewelry, and ice cream flavored with tropical fruit. For others, it is a source of life itself: The shellfish that are gathered at low tide nourish families who do not have enough money to buy such delicacies in the stores.

The beach remains busy long after sunset. The sand becomes a dance floor, a lovers' trysting spot or a place for prayer—on certain nights, devotees of the spiritist cults that first arrived with the African slave ships meet here to honor the deities of the sea.

So integral are beaches to the national way of life that, for many Brazilians, a town is only as good as its proximity to the sand and the surf. The lucky residents of Rio de Janeiro, with its 50 miles of strand, or of Salvador, with its turquoise bay and tranquil lagoons, feel only pity for the inhabitants of São Paulo and Brasília, who live inland, far from the sight or sound of the sea.

At Boca do Rio, outside Salvador, swimmers are undeterred by a turbulent surf, whipped up by stormy autumn winds. The tall trees on the dunes are among the 40 different species of coconut palm native to the coast of Brazil, once known to the Indians as the Land of Palms.

Wearing the scantiest of bikinis, known as *tangas,* two sunlovers soak up the rays on Rio de Janeiro's Copacabana Beach. Some 100,000 *cariocas—*

citizens of Rio—flock to the fashionable Copacabana each weekend, although it is just one of a dozen beaches that serve Brazil's most hedonistic city.

Against a setting of brilliant sand and wooded dunes, local women do their washing and bathe their children while a fisherman tries his luck in the waters of the Lagoa do Abaeté *(above and at right)*. The fresh-water lagoon, celebrated in folk music and art, lies about 20 miles inland from Salvador.

On Ribeira Beach, near Salvador, coast dwellers take advantage of the low tide to dig for clams and mussels in the exposed mud flats. For the poorest households, this daily harvest of shellfish is a vital source of protein, free for the taking.

An entrepreneur strides along Copacabana Beach carrying aloft an umbrella that supports an eye-catching display of headgear and dangling bottles of baby oil and suntan lotion. Behind him, white-coated vendors hawk cold drinks from metal drums.

On Copacabana Beach, in the shadow of Sugar Loaf Mountain, a young soccer player defends the goal. Professional teams stage free matches on the sand on Saturdays; during the rest of the week, youthful fans meet here to emulate their heroes.

The earliest accurate chart of Brazil, produced in 1519, shows the Portuguese flag flying north of the Amazon River (*top left-hand corner*) and south of the River Plate. Indians are depicted chopping and gathering logs of the brazilwood tree, which gave its name to the newly discovered country.

QUESTS AND CONQUESTS

On March 9, 1500, an expedition of 13 ships and 1,200 men under the command of Admiral Pedro Alvares Cabral set sail from Lisbon, Portugal, bound for India via the sea route newly established by the trail-blazing navigator, Vasco da Gama. Six weeks later, the look-outs in the fleet reported sightings of weeds and reeds in what they presumed to be midocean, and two days later, they were astonished to spy land to the westward at lat. 17° S. In this way was Brazil, now the greatest country of South America, and the fifth-largest nation on earth, "discovered" in the west by sailors who were supposed to be sailing to the east.

No one knows with certainty why Admiral Cabral's fleet, supposedly skirting Africa, should have strayed so far off course that it ended up in South America. Some suggest that it was the result of high winds or an egregious navigational error; others maintain that westward exploration was Cabral's secret intention all along. Nor is it at all certain that the Portuguese were the first Europeans to discover Brazil; both the French and the Spanish staked strong prior claims. Nevertheless, Cabral's arrival—on the 22nd of April, 1500—is taken as the moment of birth for Brazil, and the letter subsequently written to the king of Portugal by his ship's chronicler, Pero Vaz de Caminha, is recognized as the first official account of the new-found land.

Caminha's letter describes, in commendable detail and with barely restrained excitement, what the Portuguese sailors encountered when they landed at the mouth of a forested river near what is present-day Porto Seguro, between Bahia and Rio de Janeiro. Native Indians were already on the beach to meet them as they drew near in a longboat, Caminha related. "They were dark and entirely naked, with nothing to cover their private parts, and carried bows and arrows in their hands. Nicolau Coelho made a sign to them to lay down their bows, and they laid them down. He could not speak with them there because of the breaking of the sea on the shore."

After the Portuguese had landed, the two groups were touchingly friendly toward each other. The Indians danced to the lilt of the Portuguese bagpipes in a forest clearing, and later, when two of the Indian chiefs visited Cabral's flagship and fell asleep on the deck, the sailors spread a cloak over their bodies and put pillows under their heads. It is one of the great tragedies of Brazilian history that this initial attitude of mutual respect and cordiality between the two races was to be only a brief prelude to the centuries of contact and interwoven development.

Admiral Cabral's expedition spent only nine more days exploring the coast of Brazil before setting a new course for India. Although they did not stay very long, the Portuguese did two things of great symbolic significance for the future of colonialism in Brazil. One act was to hold a Christian service at which they persuaded the Indians to kneel before a huge wooden cross. The other was to leave behind two convicts who had been sentenced to death. The Portuguese viewed miscegenation as a major step toward successful colonization, and so Cabral had brought along convicts to be left to interbreed with the natives of any potential colony encountered. The two abandoned men wept in vain on the shore as the fleet weighed anchor. But then they settled down to a lifetime of procreation—the first of thousands upon thousands of Portuguese who were to change the human mix in Brazil beyond identification.

Cabral had christened the newly discovered country Terra da Vera Cruz—the Land of the True Cross. But within a few years, it was popularly known as Brazil, after the tree that soon became much sought after in Europe for the valuable, rich red dye that could be extracted from its wood. The name Terra do Brasil, the Land of the Brazilwood Tree, first appeared on a map in 1511; and for a few score years brazilwood was almost the only commodity of economic interest to come out of the country. At the time, the Portuguese were far more concerned with developing their spice trade in the Far East. But by the late 1520s, that trade had dwindled dramatically; and so, more and more, they turned their attention to the economic potential of Brazil.

The Portuguese began sending ships to patrol the Brazilian coast and fend off French and Dutch intruders. When this failed to discourage foreign rivals, they decided to establish a major settlement. In 1531, Admiral Martim Alfonso de Sousa was sent out with five ships, 400 sailors and colonists, and

2

An engraving of the 17th-century Jesuit missionary, Father António Vieira, shows him blessing two Indians recently converted to Christianity. In 1655, Vieira, a fiery preacher against the cruelty of slavery, secured a Portuguese royal decree protecting Indians from enslavement by settlers.

seeds, plants and domestic animals. The following year, he founded the coastal settlement of São Vicente near present-day Santos, and on the orders of his king, João III, he divided Brazil into 15 "captaincies," or districts, marked out at intervals of roughly 150 miles along the coast, and stretching far into the unexplored interior. Each district was granted in perpetuity to a person prominent at the Portuguese court—a feudal practice guaranteeing that the land would be colonized without expense to the royal exchequer.

Initially, the captaincies developed slowly. The distances were enormous and communications so difficult that the territories suffered from extreme isolation. They also suffered from lack of funds and lack of people. The major crop was sugar cane, along with wheat and grapes; numerous colonists also tried cattle ranching. Many plantations failed, however, while some succeeded only to be destroyed by hostile Indians or French interlopers. Portugal's Brazilian colony demanded stronger direction, and so, in 1549, the king sent out the first governor general, Tomé de Sousa, to coordinate the development and defense of the captaincies. He was accompanied by a group of Jesuit priests, who were to take charge of the religious interests of the colonists and evangelize the Indians.

The new governor general established his administration at the new town of Salvador, strategically placed midway between the far north and the far south of the country. Thereafter, new settlements sprang up in rapid succession—most notably São Paulo, founded in 1554, and Rio de Janeiro, which was established in 1565 in response to an abortive French attempt to found a colony on the shores of Gua-

nabara Bay. The white population of the colony increased from 3,000 in 1549 to 20,000 in 1570. Meanwhile, increasingly huge tracts of land were given over to the cultivation of sugar cane, especially in Pernambuco, Bahia and São Vicente, and within a decade, Brazil had become the leading sugar-producing region in the world.

Sugar plantations were voracious establishments; their appetite for land, capital and labor was seemingly insatiable. In Brazil, land abounded and capital could generally be found, but labor was scarce. There were not enough white settlers, and most of them were not inclined toward heavy physical work. The obvious solution was to press the native population into forced labor. Many Indian tribes resisted, and invariably at terrible cost as the European invaders replied with a long succession of campaigns of extermination or pacification.

The coastal tribes were the first victims of this protracted genocide. The warlike Tupinambá tribe around Rio de Janeiro and Bahia was virtually liquidated by slaughter, slavery and confinement in Jesuit missions. In Pernambuco, the Caeté were wiped out by military expeditions, and far and wide, entire villages were eliminated by epidemics of European diseases such as smallpox, measles and influenza, against which the Indians had no immunity. During the 17th century, the Indians of the interior suffered the same fate as a consequence of repeated slave-hunting expeditions.

Until they were expelled from Brazil in 1759, the Jesuits attempted to protect the Indians from the ravages of the slave hunters. They settled them in special villages where they could be Christianized and taught trades useful to colonial society. But for many years outside the Jesuit villages, the Indians continued to be rounded up and pressed into forced labor on plantations where they never remained long in service, dying of either disease or the death wish, or running away to join Indian tribes hostile to whites. There were at least two million Indians in Brazil when the Portuguese first arrived (some estimates put the figure as high as five million), but in less than a century, probably two thirds of them had been liquidated.

Statistically, the reduction in numbers among the indigenous Indians of Brazil was more or less balanced by the importation of slaves from Portugal's African colonies in Guinea and Angola. Beginning in the middle of the 16th century, ships full of slaves destined for sale to sugar-cane growers arrived on a regular basis. Many of the slaves died on the voyage, chained like animals in pestilential holds that reached furnace-like temperatures in the tropical climate. Some 30,000 Africans were estimated to have been brought in during the remainder of the 16th century, half a million during the following century, and a grand total of perhaps 3.3 million by the time the slave trade was abolished in 1850, more than 300 years after it had begun.

The African slaves were, in general, much stronger and were capable of harder work than their Indian counterparts; they were also more resistant to disease. The presence of the blacks on the plantations of the north worked wonders in terms of increased production and profits. In the south, however, plantation owners were generally unable to afford the high price for African slaves, and so they continued to exploit native Indian labor. But, black or brown, slaves were literally worked to death—or simply murdered by sadistic owners. There were cases of slaves being boiled alive in the sugar vats or castrated with razors as punishment for misdemeanors.

In Brazil, there were several harvests of sugar cane during the year, so there was scarcely any period when slaves were unprofitably idle. "A sugar mill is hell," reported the Jesuit Andrés de Gouvea in 1627, "and all the masters are damned." Like so many visitors to Brazilian sugar mills, he was appalled by the nightmarish scenes presented by the roaring furnaces, the bubbling caldrons and the eternal grinding of the mill machinery, which worked continuously, day and night.

The world of the sugar plantation was a microcosm of early colonial Brazil. Within it, the slaves represented the rock bottom of the social order, while the white planters were its aristocracy. The wealthy sugar captains generally lived on their vast estates in the *casas grandes*, or "great houses," and below them lay the cane fields, the mills, the quarters of the white and colored artisans, and the *senzalas*, or "barracks," of the slaves. But while the Brazilian whites controlled every facet of the black slaves' lives, the sheer number of the slaves profoundly influenced the formation of Brazilian society and transformed the physiognomy of the people. From the very beginning, the Portuguese settlers had been partial to the Indians, and they found the African blacks equally attractive. Slave concubines became the norm rather than the exception. The Church and polite society looked the other way. There was a great need to populate the country, so all procreation was seen as a contribution to the greater cause.

2

Many white fathers felt inclined to free their half-white offspring, along with their black mothers, so it was not long before a considerable number of free nonwhites began to take their place in Brazilian society.

Throughout the 17th century, Brazil's wealth was centered in the northeast, where the largest and most productive sugar plantations were situated. The south, by contrast, remained relatively undeveloped, and as a result, it was the southern Brazilians who were driven by economic necessity to make the most determined and daring efforts to explore deep into the interior. In doing so, they were largely responsible for the westward advancement of Brazil's frontiers, and in the end, they were to provide the means that made possible the colony's rapid development. They discovered gold.

The pioneers who blazed the trail into the interior were the so-called *bandeirantes*—the epic heroes of Brazil, tough, intrepid, rapacious members of armed bands, who set off into the untrodden wilderness beyond the coastal fringe in search of Indian slaves and precious stones and metals. The *bandeirantes* (literally "flag-bearers") were soldiers of fortune, mainly Paulistas—settlers of São Paulo. They drew into their ranks backwoodsmen from every shade of Brazil's racial mix, especially men of mixed Amerindian blood.

In a different land and a different age they might well have won praise as outstanding figures in the history of geographical exploration. They traveled enormous distances on foot or by canoe. They penetrated the mountain barriers, cut trails through the bush, followed the turbulent rivers of the vast forests, waded the swamps, pressed on across the parched scrublands, always forward into forbidding regions no outsider had seen before. But these explorers were mainly illiterate, anonymous men who left few traces in the geographical records. Wearing loose cotton trousers, broad-brimmed hats and little else, the *bandeirante* was a veritable walking arsenal—a sword and pistol in his belt, a bow in his hand, a knife hanging from his chest, a rifle and cartridge belts slung over his shoulders. He survived by mastering the bushcraft of the Indian, and became inured to hunger, thirst, fatigue and the hostility of the insects and climate. Warlike Indian tribes learned to fear such intruders.

By the early 18th century, the major settlements of Brazil had been linked by a communications network pioneered by the *bandeirantes*. Fleets of 65-foot-long dugout canoes plied the rivers. Mule trains, with as many as 50 mules, operated regular trading schedules across bush and mountains, and in the process, the *bandeirantes* not only opened up the country but helped to unify it as well. They pacified or enslaved the Indian tribes that barred westward progress, and by their discoveries of gold, they initiated the most dramatic phase in the development of their country.

Between 1693 and 1695, discoveries of alluvial gold were made in valleys of the region that is now the south-central state of Minas Gerais (General Mines). Adventurers and vagabonds from all over the colony joined in the subsequent gold rush, and before long, fleets of fortune seekers were arriving from Europe, in addition. The human flood—one without parallel until the California gold rush of 1849—continued for years, even though the overland journey to the farthest gold strikes could take seven months or more and was extremely perilous. One route, for example, involved negotiating 100 rapids, and there was always great loss of life when canoes overturned. Hostile Indians also exacted their toll: One tribe was responsible for the deaths of 600 men in a single convoy and more than 400 men in another.

Conditions in the remote, undeveloped region of the gold fields were lawless and tumultuous, and for the first decade or so, the miners were beyond the control of the colonial government. Indeed, the conflicts between rival groups of miners sometimes erupted into outright warfare. Yet the flood of dreamers of El Dorado continued for decades. Boom towns sprang up overnight, and some mining camps grew into small cities, dazzling outposts of 18th-century culture.

The lifestyle in these towns was one of enormous contrasts. The few who struck it rich were wildly ostentatious spenders. "They went about accompanied by troops of matchlock men," reported Italian Jesuit Antonil, "ready to execute any violence and to take the greatest and most frightful revenge, without any fear of the law. The gold excited them to gamble lavishly, and heedlessly to squander vast sums on vain luxuries. For instance, they would give one thousand *cruzados* for a Negro Trumpeteer; and double that for a mulatto prostitute, in order to indulge with her in continual and scandalous sins." On the other hand, luckless prospectors suffered appalling hardships in an infertile region where food prices were more than 50 times higher than those on the coast.

The gold rush played havoc with the economy of Brazil. Sugar and tobacco

plantations in the east were often abandoned in favor of the search for quick riches in the gold fields, and foodstuffs, goods, cattle, slaves and services gravitated to the mining settlements. Meanwhile, the government was unable to suppress the widespread traffic of contraband gold as miners became more and more adept at avoiding payment of the tax called the *quinto*, or "royal fifth." They were often abetted in their efforts to do this by delinquent priests who smuggled gold dust to the coast inside hollow crucifixes.

Brazil's output of precious minerals (diamonds as well as gold were eventually discovered in Mato Grosso, Goiás and Minas Gerais) reached its height in 1760. By then, nearly half the world's supply of gold was being produced by Brazil. Coming at a time of decline in Portugal's economy, these riches should have provided the Portuguese treasury with a massive boost. But some of the new wealth was misspent in Lisbon on royal and civic extravagances, and much of the rest went to London to pay off Portugal's mounting deficit in the balance of trade with the English.

In the long run, the gold cycle did not enrich either Portugal or Brazil, but because of attendant inflation, contributed to their impoverishment. Indeed, the obsession with gold brought the area of Minas Gerais to the verge of self-destruction; and in the 1770s,

2

when the gold cycle finally declined, only diversification into other economic activities, notably cattle ranching, enabled the region to survive.

There were, however, some compensations of fundamental importance. The gold rush opened up the interior and it provided a powerful impetus for the urbanization of Brazil. It also stimulated immigration on an unprecedented scale: 400,000 Portuguese left for Brazil in the 18th century, and two million slaves were shipped over from Africa—one third of them destined for the gold mines. By 1725, half the total colonial population was living in the gold region of south-central Brazil, and as a consequence, the colony's center of gravity was shifted from the northeast

to the southeast. As a result, the capital was transferred in 1763 from Salvador, where it had been for more than 200 years, to Rio de Janeiro.

The move to Rio more or less coincided with the beginning of a period of economic stagnation in Brazil, which was aggravated by the Portuguese authorities. They regarded their Brazilian possession as a milk cow; they put taxes, tithes and duties on all production and commerce, forbade manufacturing and burdened the economy with countless restrictions. It was not surprising that Brazilian-born whites deeply resented these impositions, just as, in other parts of the New World at that time, the English-speaking Americans and the creoles of Spanish Amer-

ica resented demands being made by London or Madrid.

In Minas Gerais, resentment simmered for years, culminating in 1789 in the formation of an abortive and tragic independence movement known as the Inconfidência Mineira, or Minas Conspiracy, which had as its members poets, priests, landowners, merchants and army officers. The conspiracy was led by Lieutenant Joaquim José da Silva Xavier, a young soldier popularly known as Tiradentes, or "the Toothpuller," because he also worked part time as a dentist. The conspirators were greatly inspired by the American Revolution and corresponded with Thomas Jefferson, to whom they looked for support. But the plans of their revolt were exposed. The Inconfidência Mineira was broken up; and Tiradentes was publicly hanged and quartered; his home was demolished and the site was scattered with salt to ensure, symbolically, that the land of his roots would be barren forever. Brazil had its first martyr to freedom.

Other abortive *inconfidências* followed—in Rio in 1794, Bahia in 1798 and Pernambuco in 1801. By now, Brazilian feelings had evolved from resentment of economic exploitation to a growing awareness of Brazilian national pride and identity. A few of Brazil's potential revolutionaries were republicans who wished to see the overthrow of the Portuguese Crown. However, the great majority were moderate reformers who simply wished for a better deal for the colonies. Under the circumstances, decades might have passed without fundamental change but for the indirect intervention in Brazil's affairs of one supremely ambitious foreigner—Napoleon Bonaparte.

In November of 1807, in the prelude to the Peninsular War, Napoleon's forces marched on Lisbon. To avoid falling into French hands, the prince regent of Portugal (the future King João VI), in the company of his mad mother, Queen Maria, and 15,000 members of the Portuguese court, boarded a fleet of 40 merchant vessels and, under the protection of British warships, set sail for their colony in Brazil. After a hideous, storm-racked voyage that lasted 54 days, the royal court landed in Salvador, and two months later, amid scenes of tumultuous rejoicing on the part of their Brazilian subjects, arrived in Rio de Janeiro. The prince regent immediately took over direct rule in place of his viceroy; and so the colonial capital became

a royal capital, and Rio the de facto capital of the Portuguese Empire.

This was a decisive moment in the history of Brazil. Dom João soon fell in love with his country of exile, and in due course, he set about transforming it. In Lisbon, he had seen the world from the point of view of a Portuguese in Europe. Now his outlook became Brazilianized, or Rio-centric; he began to initiate changes that the Brazilians had proposed and the Portuguese had vetoed for years. His first act was to end nearly three centuries of Portuguese mercantile monopoly by legalizing Brazilian trade with friendly nations and by establishing manufacturing industries on Brazilian soil. The impact was first felt in the capital. In 1808, only 90 foreign ships had anchored at the port of Rio de Janeiro; by 1822, the annual number had risen to 422. Most of the ships now entering Guanabara Bay were British. They brought with them every conceivable product of the Industrial Revolution, as well as aggressive British businessmen who were eager to exploit a new market.

The emporiums of the British merchants in Rio were Aladdin's caves of manufactured goods that few Brazilians had ever seen, and it was not long before the British lifestyle was modifying Brazilian customs. In Rio, particularly, the citizens acquired a taste for tea, took to eating their meals with Sheffield cutlery instead of fingers, and clothed themselves in the dark and sober garments of the bankers and mill owners of cold northern Europe— black frock coats, boots and top hats more appropriate to the London Stock Exchange than to the steaming, palm-fringed, parrot-colored world along the Tropic of Capricorn.

After the British the French came.

Following Napoleon's final eclipse at Waterloo in 1815, they poured into Rio as refugees. Their influence was less materialistic and more hedonistic than that of the British. The French set themselves up as the purveyors of life's luxuries, selling confections, rich pastries, fine wines, jewels and up-to-the-minute Paris fashions. They opened the first hotel and introduced the first à la carte menu of French haute cuisine. At least in its capital, Brazil became a more sophisticated place.

The year the French came was the year Dom João refused to go. After Napoleon's defeat, it was assumed that he would return with his court to Lisbon. Instead, he chose to stay and systematically set about hauling his adopted country into the 19th century. He founded the first newspaper, the first bank, the first military and naval academies, the first medical school, theater, library, museum and observatory. In Rio—now a city of 100,000 people and growing prosperous on coffee, an important new plantation crop for export—he founded the Botanical Gardens and introduced swimming as recreation. The streets of the city were paved, illuminated and policed. Brazil was being modernized and Europeanized; inevitably such processes had a profound effect on political conditions in the country.

In 1816, Dom João's mother died, and the prince regent was proclaimed King João VI. Five years later, he finally bowed to pressure to return to Portugal, leaving behind his son, Pedro, as prince regent. With the Crown again based in the mother country, the Portuguese began blundering efforts to turn back the clock and reduce Brazil to its former dependent colonial status. This arrogance, which culminated

In one of Brazil's great moments of history, the prince regent, Dom Pedro, raises his sword to cry "Independence or death!", thus signaling Brazil's break from Portugal. The event, captured by Brazilian artist Pedro Américo, took place on the banks of the Ipiranga in September 1822.

in the withdrawal of nearly all the gold reserves in the Bank of Brazil, was countered in the colony with rising nationalist and separatist fervor. For Dom Pedro there was a stark choice: He could head the independence movement or he could lose control of Brazil altogether.

On September 7, 1822—as every Brazilian patriot is taught from birth—the prince regent, resting on horseback beside a little stream called the Ipiranga in São Paulo, received a fresh batch of typically high-handed orders from Lisbon. He was so angry when he read them that he drew his saber from its scabbard, brandished it in the air, and let out a shout that has echoed down the generations as the famous *grito,* or "cry," of Ipiranga. *"Independência ou morte!"* he yelled. "Independence or death!" One month later, he was acclaimed emperor, and on the 1st of December, 1822, he was crowned in Rio de Janeiro with much pomp and ceremony. So began the era of the independent Brazilian Empire—and a giant step was taken toward the making of the modern nation of today.

Dom Pedro was not well cast in his newly assumed role of emperor. His personality was too wayward and mercurial, and his private life too scandalous, to befit the solemn grandeur of his office. A dissipated neurotic who also suffered from epileptic seizures, he scandalized even the broad-minded Brazilians with his amorous indiscretions and his growing litter of illegitimate children. The emperor liked to think that he was an avant-garde liberal, and in 1824, he promulgated a constitution that gave him considerable powers but—with a chamber of deputies that was indirectly elected on a lim-

ited suffrage—was still sufficiently progressive to survive for most of the 19th century. But he reigned for only nine years. During that time, he never succeeded in imposing his will on the country as a whole, and there were endless revolts and mercenary mutinies in the different regions.

In 1831, the first emperor of Brazil was forced to abdicate in favor of his son, also named Dom Pedro, who was then only five years old. In 1840, after nine years of regency, the boy was crowned, despite his youth. It marked the dawn of a new age of political and material development—comparable in some ways to another marathon reign just beginning in Queen Victoria's England. The new emperor, hardworking, liberal and cultivated, was destined to rule for almost half a century. As a constitutional monarch, Dom Pedro II had his authority theoretically limited to what was known as his "moderating power," under which he was allowed to appoint or dismiss any member of the government, prorogue Parliament or dissolve the Chamber of Deputies. Most important, however, he used this power with discretion, appointing the best men for the job regardless of their political persuasions. It can be argued that neither before nor since has Brazil been administered by men of such caliber.

Brazil's material expansion really began during Dom Pedro II's reign. More banks were opened, more foreign capital (mainly British) flowed in for commercial and industrial development. The emperor himself was keenly interested in scientific advances. He was the first person in Brazil to have his photograph taken, and he was the first to speak on the telephone. With his encouragement, the railroad era was

launched in 1859 when the first steam-powered train rumbled out of Rio toward the emperor's summer residence at Petropolis. In 1874, Dom Pedro went down to the beach at Copacabana—then an uninhabited stretch of sand—to inaugurate an underwater cable between Rio and London.

He served his country well for almost 50 years. Under his enlightened and responsible rule, economic production increased tenfold and public revenues fourteenfold. There remained, however, one major blot on his reign: the continuation of slavery. Dom Pedro believed that slavery was an abomination, but at the same time, he was not prepared to stand behind its immediate abolition because he feared the econom-

ic, social and political consequences.

The slave trade from Africa had been declared illegal in 1831 and was brought to an end in 1850, but there was no law against the continued ownership of slaves in Brazil. By the 1880s, emancipation had become the greatest issue of the age. Many Brazilians were deeply ashamed that theirs was the only Christian nation that still permitted slavery; even the army protested at being ordered to pursue runaways, and several states took the unilateral decision to liberate their slaves. Clearly this 300-year-old institution was doomed. But the plantation aristocracy would not capitulate, and the emperor delayed.

In 1887, tired and diabetic, the emperor went to Europe for a holiday.

The abolitionists, headed by Dom Pedro's own daughter, Princess Isabel, who was now acting as regent, seized their chance. On May 13, 1888—a quarter of a century after slavery had been abolished in the United States and 55 years after it had been abolished in the British colonies—the princess signed the "Golden Law," freeing all slaves in Brazil without compensation to their owners.

"You have redeemed a race but lost a crown," the princess was warned by the landowners. They meant what they said. Some rich planters were ruined, and in their ruin and their wrath, they turned against the monarchy and gave their support to a republican movement of middle-class businessmen and

THE AMAZON RIVER'S VORACIOUS PREDATOR

The piranha's menace is captured in a drawing (left) published in an 1829 book by naturalists J. B. de Spix and Louis Agassiz. Among the many vivid descriptions of this fresh-water hunter is one by President Theodore Roosevelt, who visited Amazonia in 1913. "The head," he wrote, "with its short muzzle, staring and malignant eyes and gaping, cruelly armed jaws, is the embodiment of ferocity." One species reaches two feet, but most are less than one foot long. They travel in large schools and chiefly attack other fish, whose flesh they tear with sharp, triangular teeth.

Nothing attracts piranha faster than blood, and an attacking school, which can number hundreds of fish, makes short shrift of large wounded animals. One school of piranha reportedly reduced a 100-pound capybara to a skeleton in less than a minute.

disaffected elements of the army who were angry with the emperor because he insisted they stay out of politics. Unaware of these rumblings, the emperor returned to Brazil and a warm welcome from the majority of his subjects. But within weeks a conspiracy against him was hatched by the army: On November 15, 1889, a republic was proclaimed, and two days later, the emperor was sent into exile with his family. In 1891, the country's last emperor died forlornly but without recrimination in a second-class hotel room in Paris.

Until 1894, the new republic of Brazil was ruled by a provisional government under a military autocracy. It made some crucially important decisions, including the separation of Church and State and the adoption of a constitution modeled on that of the United States. By the dawn of the 20th century, however, it was becoming clear that the shift to a federal republic and presidential rule had brought about little change in Brazil's basic political and social institutions.

Because suffrage was based on literacy, the mass of the people in Brazil remained outside the political process, and of the 20 to 30 percent of the population thought to be entitled to vote in municipal, state and national elections, only about 3 percent bothered to do so. Also, because power had been decentralized and given to the states, big landowners exercised enormous influence, particularly in the states of São Paulo and Minas Gerais, where political and economic power was concentrated. Most significantly, the military had become more and more politically active as they asserted their claim to being guarantors of the constitutional process and served as a check on civilian administrations.

The most dramatic changes at this time occurred in the agricultural economy. Following the decline in gold mining, coffee began to rival and then to overtake sugar cane as the outstanding export crop and source of government revenue. Meanwhile, Brazil was profiting increasingly from a natural resource that had remained untapped until 1839, when the American Charles Goodyear had invented the rubber vulcanizing process. Rubber trees grew wild in great abundance throughout the Amazon valley—an estimated 300 million trees in almost two million square miles of forest. And the demand for rubber increased sharply with the advent of automobiles and rubber tires.

By the 20th century, the Amazonian region was providing the rubber for most of the world's cars.

The center of the rubber boom became Manaus, which was the capital of Amazonas State but was a small town isolated in the heart of the rain forest 1,000 miles upstream from the Atlantic. Yet, by the early 1900s, it had grown into one of the grandest and most extravagant places on the whole continent. "I found a village," boasted the state governor of the time, "and made of it a modern city." Manaus had the first electrified public transportation service in South America and the first telephone system in the Amazon. There were hospitals and banks and pool rooms, a racecourse and a bull ring, the Grand Hotel—"the finest in Christendom"—and even a lavishly decorated opera house.

Rubber, quite simply, made Manaus the new Babylon of Brazil. There were nightspots galore and brothels where women from every country of Europe and the Orient were available at staggering prices. At private parties in the luxurious villas and palaces of the rubber kings, naked girls took showers in iced Cordon Rouge, and on such nights a tycoon thought nothing of lighting a cigar with a 500 milreis note, the equivalent today of about $150. The new rich sent their laundry to Lisbon and their children to expensive boarding schools in Switzerland and France. They ordered their marble columns from Italy, their furniture from London, their vegetables from Brussels and their opera singers from Milan.

By the early teens, rubber was almost the equal of coffee as Brazil's main source of foreign currency, and some 5,000 people a week were still swarming into Manaus to seek their fortunes

A CHRONOLOGY OF KEY EVENTS

c. 10,000 B.C. Hunter-gatherers from North America reach Brazil. They gradually settle in widely dispersed tribal grounds and develop their cultures.

1494 The Treaty of Tordesillas divides the New World—discovered and undiscovered—between Spain and Portugal.

1500 The navigator Pedro Álvares Cabral *(below)* sights the Brazilian coast and lands to claim the region for Portugal.

1532 Portuguese settlers establish their first colony at São Vicente.

1534 Brazil is divided into 15 captaincies—hereditary land grants later to become administrative units.

1538 The Portuguese start to import African slaves *(below)* to work on their sugar plantations.

1549 The newly founded city of Salvador becomes the seat of Brazil's colonial government.

1554 The Jesuits establish a mission at São Paulo.

1600 Expeditions into the interior by hard-bitten settlers known as *bandeirantes* begin to extend Brazil's territory westward. *Bandeirantes* repeatedly clash with Jesuits protecting the Indians from slavery and exploitation.

1639 Portugal claims the Amazon basin.

1654 The expulsion of Dutch settlers from Brazil marks the end of a succession of attempts by other nations—including Britain and France—to gain a share of Portugal's South American discoveries.

1680 Brazil expands southward to the River Plate and comes into conflict with Spain over Uruguay.

1693 Gold is found in the hinterland, initiating a century-long gold rush.

1750 Spain and Portugal settle Brazilian border disputes by the Treaty of Madrid.

1754 Brazil's administrative structure is revised, with the abolition of the hereditary captaincies.

1759 The Jesuits are banished.

1763 Rio de Janeiro *(above)* becomes the capital of Brazil.

1789 An independence plot led by Joaquim José da Silva Xavier, nicknamed Tiradentes (the Toothpuller) is crushed by authorities.

1805 O Aleijadinho (Antônio Francisco Lisbôa) completes a series of statues for the Sanctuary of Bom Jesus near Ouro Prêto.

1808 To escape Napoleon's invasion of Portugal, the Portuguese Prince Regent João transfers his court to the Brazilian capital of Rio de Janeiro.

1816 The prince regent succeeds to the Portuguese throne as João VI.

1821 King João is recalled to Portugal to deal with the ferment left by the Napoleonic Wars. His son, Dom Pedro, remains as regent.

1822 Provoked by reactionary attitudes in Portugal, Dom Pedro proclaims Brazil's independence, becoming emperor.

1824 Brazil receives a constitution on the liberal United States pattern.

1831-1840 The abdication of Pedro I leads to a decade of disorder and civil war under a regency, ending with the accession of Pedro II, aged 14, as emperor. His enlightenment and concern during a 49-year reign bring tremendous social and cultural advances.

1845 Coffee (below) introduced in the 18th century, accounts for almost half Brazil's export earnings.

1887 Heitor Villa-Lobos, Brazil's greatest composer, is born in Rio.

1888 Slavery is abolished.

1889 A military plot, fueled by growing republican sentiment, secures Pedro's abdication and the end of the monarchy. A provisional regime adopts a presidential republican constitution in 1891.

1893 Opposition to dictatorial rule by military presidents leads to unrest and, in 1894, to the election of Brazil's first civilian president.

1896 The Manaus Opera House, symbol of the short-lived Amazonian rubber boom, is opened. World demand for rubber began with the invention of vulcanizing in 1839.

1913 The Brazilian rubber boom suddenly dies as a result of competition from the Far East.

SEMANA·DE·ARTE· MODERNA ~ CATALOGO

1917 Brazil enters World War I in support of the Allies; pelo telefone, the first samba ever recorded, becomes popular.

1922 A Week of Modern Art (catalogue above) in São Paulo triggers a period of sustained, intense literary and artistic activity.

1929 Worldwide economic depression damages the Brazilian economy when coffee prices collapse.

1930 Gathering social and political unrest leads to a revolt headed by young military officers. Getúlio Vargas, governor of the state of Rio Grande do Sul, comes to power.

1937 Getúlio Vargas (right) seizes absolute power.

1942 Brazil enters World War II on the side of the Allies.

1945 In a bloodless coup, a group of army officers force Vargas to resign. The following year, Brazil reverts to a democratic constitution.

1950 Vargas is re-elected president. His term of office is marked by economic difficulties.

1954 His administration rocked by scandals, Vargas resigns and commits suicide on the same day.

1956 Juscelino Kubitschek, elected president in 1955, takes office and promises to achieve "50 years of progress in five."

1960 The new city of Brasília is declared the capital of Brazil.

1964 After the left-wing government's controversial legislation has alienated conservatives, a military coup establishes a dictatorship.

1973 Brazil's economic progress is crowned by the achievement of the world's fastest rate of economic growth for the year: 14 percent.

1980 The overheated Brazilian economy crashes, leaving Brazil the world's greatest debtor nation.

1984 The Itaipu Dam, the world's largest, opens near the Brazilian border with Paraguay.

1985 Brazil returns to civilian government.

1987 Newly appointed Finance Minister Luiz Carlos Bresser Pereira devalues the cruzeiro against the U.S. dollar, improving Brazil's ability to repay its $108-billion foreign debt.

2

in a city with a population that had grown to more than one million souls. Nobody knew it at the time, but the whole edifice of their prosperity was already beginning to crumble. Many years earlier, in 1876, the English botanist Henry Wickham had collected rubber tree seeds in the Amazon valley, which he had successfully propagated in London's Kew Gardens. The young trees grown from the seeds were then transferred to British plantations in the Far East, where they matured and were ready for tapping.

In 1913, the price of rubber fell to less than a quarter of the record price it had commanded in 1910. The following year, the Far Eastern plantations put 72,546 tons of rubber on the market, and the price slumped still further. Many powerful Amazonian families went bankrupt immediately, and mass emigration southward began. All along the great river, buildings stood empty and abandoned; cattle were penned in former drawing rooms among the rotting grand pianos and rusting harps; in Manaus, the street lights went out because the municipality could no longer afford to pay for electricity. The bonanza was over.

In these depressing economic circumstances, the outbreak of World War I was timely, bringing as it did an increased demand for Brazilian coffee, rubber and sugar. Brazil remained neutral until October 26, 1917; then, following German attacks on its shipping, it supported the Allies with naval units and considerable supplies of food and raw materials. During the war years, the volume of industrial production doubled, and by 1923, it had tripled. In turn, industrialization brought about greatly increased urbanization of cities such as São Paulo and encouraged the rise of a new industrial proletariat and middle class.

New skills and trades were brought to the cities by immigrant workers from Europe, who had started arriving in Brazil in the days of the late empire. The Japanese began to arrive in 1908, swelling the influx, and before the outbreak of World War I, annual immigration had reached record levels—500,000 newcomers between 1911 and 1913. The new arrivals—mainly from Italy, Portugal and, to a lesser extent, from Spain, Germany, Poland and the Levant—continued to flow into Brazil until the 1930s, by which time some five million people born outside the country were estimated to have entered. Although the immigrant population never exceeded more than 6 percent of the Brazilian-born population, the energy and new ideas they brought with them made a disproportionate impact on the economy and lifestyle of their adopted country, which remained for the most part a poor, rural and illiterate nation.

As late as the 1920s, about 70 percent of the Brazilian population worked on the land—land that was owned and largely governed by a privileged oligarchy whose wealth was now founded on the coffee industry. But there was a new atmosphere: A passionate nationalist pride was emerging in a new generation of idealistic intellectuals, civilians and soldiers alike, who repudiated the past and championed the forces for reform and change.

Young military officers—the *tenentes*, or "lieutenants"—formed the most vociferous and effective opposition group. Without any ambition for personal power, they saw themselves as the guardians of the constitution. They wanted the establishment of a broadly based electorate, social legislation, agrarian reform, nationalization of the mines, recognition for labor unions, and free primary and technical education throughout the country; they also wanted an end to the power monopoly of the coffee oligarchy, as well as an end to corruption, fraud, injustice, censorship and repression by the government. Last, they wanted a strong central government for a united Brazil and an end to the growing separatist tendency of the regional states.

The officers struck their first blow after the 1922 presidential elections. In Rio, a small group of them staged a revolt at the military fort on Copacabana Beach. When they came under bombardment from military units loyal to the government, 18 of them—known as the Copacabana 18—made a last stand on the beach and were gunned down almost to a man. Although the rebellion ended in disaster, it initiated a series of army revolts that ultimately lead to the overthrow of the republic in 1930. By then, the entire world was experiencing the Great Depression. Coffee prices were plummeting, the Brazilian export market had shriveled and the exchange rate was at a record low. São Paulo, as the leading coffee state, was the region most affected, and this meant that its coffee oligarchy was more vulnerable to attack.

The attack came when the powerful states of Minas Gerais and Rio Grande do Sul aligned themselves with the rebellious military element and other disaffected groups in a coalition they called the Liberal Alliance. Their nominee for president was the stocky, dynamic governor of the southern state of Rio Grande do Sul, Getúlio Vargas, who stood for modernization and reform. When Vargas lost the election, the military revolted. An army junta

seized control of the government, and insurrectionary troops marched toward the capital from the north and the south, unseating each of the state governors in their turn. Vargas, in the meantime, journeyed to Rio in triumph, enthusiastically acclaimed by everyone who saw in him a symbol of revolutionary change, and in November of 1930, the junta proclaimed Vargas president. Thus the old republic ended as it had begun—as the consequence of military intervention.

Getúlio Vargas was 47 years old when he assumed power in Brazil and 71 when he relinquished it by the expediency of putting a bullet through his heart. His rule—first as a constitutional president elected by Congress, then as a self-appointed dictator, and finally as a constitutional president chosen by the people—lasted nearly a quarter of a century, with an intermission of five years after the end of the Second World War. Although his reputation was hotly disputed, his legacy to Brazil was undoubtedly tremendous.

At first Vargas made positive concessions to the *tenentes* who had helped him to power. But the honeymoon with radical elements of the army was short-lived. In 1932, insurgents in the state of São Paulo, convinced that Vargas was preparing to establish a military dictatorship, rose up against him and were crushed. A new "strongman" had emerged in Brazil, just as other strong-

men were emerging in the totalitarian states of Europe. Two years later, a new constitution was promulgated; it gave the central government greater powers over the regional states and incorporated many of the democratic demands of the revolutionaries, including the secret ballot, the representation of all classes in Congress, and female suffrage. Vargas also established labor unions in the factories, brought them under state control, and imposed a minimum wage and maximum work week. Child labor was outlawed and women were given the same wage rights as men. These were the first measures ever taken to close the immense gap between rich and poor in Brazil, and they naturally won Vargas support

OUTLAWS OF THE BRAZILIAN BACK COUNTRY

The bandit leader sits for a 1926 portrait.

Lampião's gang and two camp followers don their finery for the photographer.

among the masses. But Vargas was no democrat. In November of 1937, while the country was preparing for presidential elections, Vargas staged a coup: He surrounded the two houses of Congress with troops and put into effect a new constitution that gave him virtually absolute power.

The new regime, known as the Estado Novo, or New State, bore certain similarities to Mussolini's corporative state in Fascist Italy and Salazar's Estado Novo in Portugal. Vargas announced that 20th-century democracy was decadent and defunct. "The Estado Novo," he declared, "does not recognize the rights of the individual against the collective. Individuals do not have rights; they have duties. Rights belong to the collective!" At this point, there was so much power con-

centrated in Vargas' hands that he was able to suppress all manifestations of democracy and the popular will. Political parties were banned, newspapers censored and opponents imprisoned.

Critics of Vargas' regime called it "fascism with sugar," but his dictatorship did not descend to the worst barbarities of his European counterparts. There were no concentration camps and no mass murders, and most political prisoners were soon released and allowed to go into exile. Nor was there any great confusion in Vargas' mind as to where his sympathies lay when World War II began. Loyal to the concept of Pan-Americanism, he followed the United States' lead. After the Japanese attack on Pearl Harbor, he opened Brazilian ports and airfields to the U.S. armed forces; and in August

1942, after several Brazilian merchant ships had been torpedoed by German U-boats in the South Atlantic, he declared war on the Axis powers, a decision greeted with popular rejoicing.

In a great contribution to the Allied war effort, the Brazilian navy took responsibility for all patrol duties in the South Atlantic, allowing the United States' warships to be concentrated in the Far East; and in July 1944, a Brazilian expeditionary force of 25,000 men joined the U.S. 5th Army in Italy, where it distinguished itself in several battles, especially at Monte Castello, and suffered nearly 2,500 casualties. One year later, the troops returned to a heroes' welcome. The war had established Brazil as a leader in the South American community and ensured the country a place of honor in the United

Of the many bandits roaming the back country of northeastern Brazil, the most notorious was Lampião (the Lantern), who terrorized six states in the 1920s and 1930s. Leading a large company of outlaws, he attacked individuals, ranches, even entire towns. Although his crimes included rape, arson, robbery, torture and murder, Lampião's occasional humane gestures—returning a robbery victim's wedding ring or giving to the poor—earned him the reputation of a Robin Hood. His exploits were glamorized in poems, books, and even a documentary.

After 16 years of evading capture, Lampião was shot by government troops in 1938. His head, exhibited as proof of his death, was an attraction in a Salvador museum until 1969.

Nations. It had given a massive boost to Brazilian agriculture, to mining of minerals needed as war matériel, and to manufacturing industries. It had introduced army officers to the American "can-do" attitude and technology. And, indirectly, it had destroyed Vargas' political credibility.

Toward the end of the war, a group of prominent citizens in Minas Gerais had declared: "If we fight against fascism at the side of the United States so that liberty and democracy may be restored to all people, certainly we are not asking too much in demanding for ourselves such rights and guarantees." The army concurred and put pressure on Vargas to set a date for free elections and a return to democracy. In October 1945, when it appeared that Vargas was planning to mobilize popular support and remain in power in perpetuity, a group of high-ranking officers demanded that he resign. Thus, the Estado Novo, like the empire and the republic before it, was ended by the intervention of a self-appointed guardian of public morality—the military.

Yet many Brazilians mourned the downfall of Vargas, for his regime had pioneered social legislation that had helped to alleviate the lot of the urban proletariat and had given them a sense of national identity for the first time in their history. It had reformed the educational system, diversified agriculture, and by the establishment of the steel mills at Volta Redonda and industrial development elsewhere, it had laid the foundation of a more sound economy for the future.

Such a record of achievement was sufficient to ensure that Vargas did not disappear completely from the political arena. He staged his comeback in 1950, following five years of honest and relatively liberal government under the presidency of General Eurico Gaspar Dutra. As leader of a new political front, the Brazilian Labor Party, Vargas successfully aimed his presidential election campaign at the working class and the rural landowners, and in January 1951, he was once again installed in the presidential palace in Rio.

This time, however, it seemed that there could be no return to his pre-1945 style of government, and until 1953, Vargas attempted to abide by the new democratic constitution, which had been drawn up in 1946. But members of his administration were profoundly corrupt, and they eventually aroused the wrath of the military.

The crisis came in 1954, when Brazilian journalist Carlos Lacerda attempted to expose the most blatant examples of government graft. In an attempt to assassinate Lacerda, Vargas' bodyguard shot Lacerda's bodyguard, who was an air force major. The political murder put the entire nation in an uproar, which was all the more intense because of rumors that Vargas was plotting to seize power on a more permanent basis. A delegation of senior army officers demanded the president's resignation.

It was early on the morning of the 24th of August when Vargas, who was still in his pajamas, agreed to the officers' demand. He then retired to his bedroom to pen an open letter to the Brazilian people: "I can give nothing further but my blood. I choose this way to be always with you. I gave you my life. Now I offer my death. Serenely I take the first step on the road to eternity and leave my life to enter history." Some people claim that the letter is the work of another hand, but there seems no doubt that it was Vargas' finger on the trigger of the pistol that buried a bullet in his heart.

After a short period of interim government, Juscelino Kubitschek, a former governor of the state of Minas Gerais, whom many regarded as Vargas' political heir, came to power in January 1956. Kubitschek was a man of great personal charisma, restless energy and driving ambition, and he was determined to catapult his country to the forefront of the world's nations. "Fifty years' progress in five!" was his slogan, and the industrialization of Brazil was thrown into high gear. Enormous dams were constructed to help meet the increased demand for electrical power; the automobile industry was started up, and iron-ore exports were doubled: It was a model of industrial growth built on an alliance of state

2

planning and foreign and private capital. Then, on a bleak, almost treeless wilderness on the central plateau of Brazil, Kubitschek gave the order for work to begin on the creation of the Brazilian dream—the construction of the new capital of Brasília. This formidable undertaking was to serve a dual purpose for Kubitschek: It would mark a major step in Brazil's historic march into the interior, and it would ensure for himself an immortal niche in the country's history.

Responsibility for the design of all government buildings in the new capital fell to Kubitschek's personal friend, Brazilian architect Oscar Niemeyer. The 100,000 workers who were brought into the wild and desolate location in the state of Goiás worked around the clock to complete the project within the five-year term of the Kubitschek presidency. Since there was no rail line, and the only roads were made of dirt and were subject to seasonal flooding, all the raw materials, including cement, were airlifted to the construction site—at astronomical cost. It was typical of the way in which the ebullient—and visionary—Kubitschek shrugged aside the tremendous practical and financial obstacles that threatened this herculean labor.

In April 1960, amid rapturous celebration, the new capital was officially inaugurated. It had cost more than one billion dollars and it was still not finished. Indeed, many members of the federal bureaucracy could find nowhere to live in Brasília, and some senior civil servants were making the 1,700-mile round-trip commute between the old capital and the new capital every working day. Brasília, it seemed, had brought the nation to the brink of bankruptcy, and inflation now began to spiral toward giddy heights in an economy superheated by uncontrolled industrial expansion. Moreover, government corruption and waste had not diminished. In the south of the country, political and economic power remained in the hands of the minority; in the north, the people were still abysmally poor.

In January 1961, when Kubitschek stepped down from the presidency, he left behind him a nation in a state of financial chaos. His critics said that instead of "50 years' progress in five," he had achieved "40 years' inflation in four." Kubitschek's two presidential successors, Jânio Quadros and João Goulart, were destined to founder on Brazil's economic rocks, and neither served a full five-year term of office. The same economic forces contributed to the chaos that resulted in the army generals' coup of 1964 and, 21 years later, to the restoration of democracy by a military government whose illusions of economic grandeur had rebounded on them.

But Kubitschek's historic legacy remained. Brasília—as modernistic as a space city but as inconvenient as a frontier town, a pioneer's dream and a pedestrian's nightmare—stood foursquare under the skies of the great central plateau. Shaped like a bird or a plane—or like a drawn bow aimed into the interior—Brasília was the symbol of a new future and a nation reborn.

Whatever troubles still lay ahead in the 1960s, Brasília provided the irresistible impulse that would open up the sparsely inhabited and underdeveloped wilderness of the interior and unite its disjointed parts, so that one day the Brazilian nation would be able to fulfill its promise as *o país do futuro*—the land of the future. ☐

Standing on a newly cleared tract of land in 1957, surveyors lay out the plan of Brasília, which three years later was inaugurated as the new capital of Brazil. The project included building an 18-mile-long lake and a yacht club, as well as houses and government and commercial centers.

Two jubilant young Brazilians wave their national flag during the 1985 election campaign. The slogan "Order and Progress" is emblazoned across a map of the night sky as seen from Rio: The constellation of 23 stars represents the states of the federal republic and the unity of the people.

RICH AND POOR, BLACK AND WHITE

In his seminal work *The Masters and the Slaves,* the Brazilian sociologist Gilberto Freyre documented the crucial role of plantation society in the development of Brazilian civilization. "Like a powerful god," he concluded, it "divided us into enslaver and enslaved." In 1934, when Freyre's book was published, slavery had been abolished in Brazil for nearly half a century, but its heritage was still apparent everywhere. A network of wealthy landowners continued to wield immense power; the black exslaves, for the most part, remained firmly on the bottom-most rung of a steep social ladder.

Since the 1930s—and especially since the 1960s—industrialization, urbanization and massive population growth have profoundly altered the shape of this society. Seventy percent of Brazilians now live in cities. The masters of old have been replaced by a burgeoning middle class, which today numbers some 30 million. A manufacturing working class has come into being. Yet still discernible within the new outlines of the country's class structure are the quintessentially Brazilian features that Freyre pinpointed. Disparities in wealth and position are still enormous. Individuals from good families gain disproportionate influence through their assiduously cultivated connections. And most blacks are still found among the poor.

At the pinnacle of the social scale, the descendants of the slave-owning aristocrats live on in their spacious colonial houses on the coffee and sugar plantations. Often their lifestyle is quite simple; even in the colonial era, enormous fortunes were rarely made in Brazil, and what wealth a family once possessed may well have been dissipated by now. But the country landowners wield power, especially in the north and northeast. Their tenants, and the tradespeople who depend on them, defer to their political views and vote according to their direction.

Often the landowners own local newspapers, and in this way, they are able to mold the opinions of a wider circle of country people than those with whom they have direct dealings. The landowners frequently have a hand in appointments in the police and the judiciary. They maximize their impact on regional politics through complex webs of family connections.

In Brazil's colonial days, the *parentela*—or extended family—came to embrace not just blood relations but also in-laws, adopted children and godchildren. The patriarch of a family would use the *parentela* to consolidate his interests, marrying his daughters to wealthy neighbors, securing powerful godfathers for his sons. Once recruited thus into his sphere, they could be expected to act in his interests. These days, young Brazilian women—even those from traditional-minded families—expect to make up their own minds about whom they will marry. But

3

family continues to command powerful loyalties among the rural aristocracy.

To be a member of the urban establishment—the band of powerful business leaders, civil servants and professionals who make up perhaps 5 percent of the population—does not always require family connections nowadays. Taking advantage of the opportunities provided by the economic miracle, a few talented men have climbed to the top without benefit of family. Most of the newcomers are the ambitious and hardworking descendants of fairly recent immigrants—the Italians, Japanese, Czechoslovakians and others who arrived in the early years of this century looking for opportunities in a land of

potential. But the majority among the wealthy and powerful are not first-generation success stories. They come from families comfortably established for several decades.

The urban elite sets great store by education. Virtually every child is expected to aim for a university education. From the late 1960s, Brazil's university system—consisting of both state-funded and private colleges—expanded hugely. In the course of the 1970s, the student capacity of undergraduate institutions increased from fewer than half a million to more than a million, of graduate institutions from 3,000 to 38,000. Many young adults study abroad for a few years after get-

ting a first degree at a Brazilian university. They arrive home with masters' degrees and doctorates from famous European and North American institutions and glide smoothly into high-powered jobs in industry, government or the professions.

Qualifications, however, are not their only weapons in the struggle for success. Anyone who has strings to pull does so—and to a far greater extent than is usual in the United States and Europe. When somebody lands a plum job, a natural question for friends to ask is, "Who got you into it?" Very often the answer is an uncle or a godfather—evidence that the *parentela* is still integral to the functioning of urban Brazil.

64

Many among the new breed of superbly educated Brazilians, meritocrats on the surface, turn out on close acquaintance to have a connection with one of the country's old lineages. Family ties mean a great deal to such people. The history and traditions of their line are compelling topics of conversation. They stay in regular contact with distant cousins and in-laws. For some, attending baptisms, weddings, confirmation services and other family events occupies so much time that outside contacts are difficult to maintain.

Professional salaries are very uneven in Brazil. A top civil servant whose uncle is a minister will earn a large salary. An ordinary administrator will be badly paid. A fashionable doctor can easily earn five times as much as one with a modest practice in an undistinguished part of town. But salaries at the top in Brazil are high by any standard, and members of the upper middle class live better than their counterparts in most other countries. Many have a house on an estate in the country as well as a fashionable apartment in town. They belong to clubs where they can play tennis or golf, swim or eat in exclusive company—often with their membership fee paid by their employers. They relax at away-from-it-all beach resorts and travel widely as tourists within Brazil. They often spend their Saturdays shopping in huge multistory malls built along American lines.

At a more intimate level, as well, lifestyles are much like those in North America and Western Europe. For all their concern with the ramifications of kin, the Brazilian elite live as nuclear families in their city apartments. The women usually marry young, the men rather later. Divorce was legalized only in 1977, but already it carries little stigma. Nor is there overwhelming social pressure to remarry: For second and subsequent unions, couples often just live together. Portuguese has the same word for "wife" and "woman," so at social gatherings it is easy for men to gloss over the legal status of a relationship. Many of the Brazilians engaged in the hectic search for fulfilling relationships are as fascinated with psychoanalysis as any stereotypical New Yorker or Californian is.

But there are differences as well, perhaps the most striking of which is the availability of servants in Brazil. Domestic workers are important as status symbols, and a great deal of social gossip consists of minute assessments of the merits and failings of household staff. The average well-to-do family has two female servants—usually black—one of whom lives in. Even members of the lower middle class—shop owners, clerical workers and the like—customarily have a maid.

One third of the women employed in Brazil are in domestic service, acting as nannies, cooks and cleaning maids. Those who live in are given a small bedroom close to the kitchen. Although they are allowed a siesta in the afternoon, they have little time they can call entirely their own. They are often paid less than the meager legal minimum wage—in theory the amount necessary to keep a family of four, although in practice it falls considerably short of that. However, like the house slaves of the early plantation days, the domestic workers very often have a close relationship with the families they serve and, in particular, play an important role in the upbringing of their employers' children.

Thanks to the ubiquitous servants, upper-middle-class Brazilian women never have to concern themselves with chores such as cooking or cleaning. Many live a life of leisure and self-indulgence. They spend their time tanning themselves on the beach, paying daily visits to the hairdresser and shopping in stylish boutiques.

In marked contrast to this pampered breed are Brazil's professional women, who, though relatively few in number, hold key positions in commerce, academia and the law. Like their brothers, they are formidably well educated, often at foreign universities. When these women step into senior jobs, they are effective and highly regarded. Many of them support Brazil's well-organized feminist movement.

Feminism came late to Brazil. In colonial days, women's only roles were those of wife and mother, and they led lives of severe seclusion. Their status did begin to change in this century when the development of new service industries provided a springboard for women to enter the labor market. In 1907, women of "good social condition" were admitted as telephone operators in Rio de Janeiro, and in 1917, the first women were allowed to join the civil service. In 1934, women were granted the vote. But Brazil was only a fringe combatant in World War II and therefore missed the impetus that the war afforded elsewhere for a reevaluation of women's capabilities. It was not until the 1970s that women became more independent, primarily because of the job opportunities that were created by economic growth and the spreading use of contraception.

In São Paulo and other major cities, modern Western feminism began to make an impact at this time. International Women's Year in 1975 led to the setting up of the Center for the Devel-

3

opment of the Brazilian Woman, which began investigating women's and children's health issues. At the same time there appeared many voluntary organizations concerning themselves with community problems such as sanitation, education and housing. Such campaigns cut across class barriers: Working-class women, often encouraged by the Catholic Church, gained confidence through their participation in local activist groups.

It was in spite of the opposition of the Catholic Church, however, that General Ernesto Geisel, a Lutheran who was

president of Brazil from 1974 to 1979, gave the government's official support to family-planning programs in the cities. For both religious and nationalistic reasons, the country had been very reluctant to do anything to discourage population growth; but when President Geisel's Roman Catholic successor, President Figueiredo, spoke about the need for "responsible parenthood," the message for women was clear. The 1980 census showed that the birth rate had dropped markedly.

Despite the newfound confidence of female professionals and women in the

upper classes, old attitudes regarding the roles of men and women are dying hard. Many Brazilian men have trouble taking the new professional women seriously. One manifestation of the old attitude toward women is the inordinate importance placed on their appearance at work. Advertisements for female staff specify good looks and youth as essentials. The majority of Brazilian women, far from resenting the requirement as sexist, cheerfully play the game. But, their insouciance may dissolve around the age of 35, and the enormous emphasis on youth can

make them terrified of the first wrinkle. Brazil has a plastic surgery industry to rival Florida's.

Another area where feminism and traditional values combine uneasily is the issue of domestic servants. Many well-to-do feminists consider it wrong in principle to keep other women in such a dependent situation and to pay them so little. Some feel so embarrassed about their exploitative position that, when circles of feminists meet in private apartments, they take care not to raise the issue of domestics until the servant has retired to her room. But in practice, the development of such women's careers is underpinned by the existence of maids and child-care workers; they would have difficulty managing on their own, and few of them try. Other feminists salve their conscience by telling themselves that, despite all the injustices of the situation, poor women want the jobs and it is therefore their duty to provide employment.

Meanwhile, feminist ideas are beginning to filter through to the maids themselves. In the big cities, domestic servants are beginning to band together in small groups in order to press for such improvements as the government minimum wage, a day off a week and the right to unionize.

Domestic servants make up just a fraction of the great mass of Brazilians who endure poverty. The middle class accounts for less than a quarter of the population. Ninety million Brazilians live in conditions ranging from basic but cheerful to appalling destitution.

Some of the worst deprivation is experienced in the remote rural areas. In the northeast, the masses scratch a precarious subsistence from small family patches of parched earth with a few

Favela houses cling to the steep granite hillsides of Rio de Janeiro (*opposite*) and perch on stilts in the mud flats of Salvador (*above*). Some are solidly built, boasting power lines and television aerials, but their foundations are precarious: Landslides and floods can cause devastation.

3

corn plants and perhaps half a dozen chickens. The people are fortunate if they have meat to eat even three times in a year. Although there are mining and petrochemical projects in the region, they employ only a small number of skilled workers. The majority still depend for their cash income on day labor on the plantations at pitifully low wages. They are heavily dependent on the plantation owners for patronage, and for assistance if they run into trouble with the law. They live in shacks constructed from whatever materials they are able to scrape together. The 1980 census showed that only 17 percent of homes in the northeast had electricity, compared with two thirds in the southeast; only 1 in 10 homes had sewer service, compared with 7 out of 10 in the southeast; and only 1 in 5 had running water, compared with more than half in the southeast.

It is not surprising that the rural poor have been flocking to the cities in search of a better life. The migration to the urban areas began as early as the 1930s and later accelerated sharply with the rapid industrial growth of the

1960s and 1970s. Brazilians, like so many others, see the cities as places of hope: They crave the bright lights, the chance of quick cash. They like the noise and activity—*movimento,* as they call it admiringly.

For millions of people, the move from the countryside brought its rewards. The miracle decade of the 1970s brought upward mobility to almost everybody who found employment. The proportion of the work force who earned the minimum wage or less dropped from almost two thirds to slightly more than one third.

The gains must be seen in perspective. Although the elite of the new working class—employees in the car factories of São Paulo, for example—earn between two and five times the minimum wage, international automobile manufacturers still find them cheap to employ. More than 60 percent of the working population still earns less than twice the minimum wage—which, by developed nations' standards, means they are poor. What is more, recession in the 1980s has thrown many out of work—hence the

ready availability of domestic workers—besides slowing progress for nearly all the others. And many have merely exchanged rural for urban misery, without bettering themselves at all. To those for whom the bright lights of the cities have proved a mirage, there is nowhere else to go, no hope.

The history of two of the new city dwellers, Luís and Teotista, illustrates the possibilities and pitfalls that await countryfolk prepared to try their luck in the cities. Luís and Teotista used to be neighbors in the northeastern state of Pernambuco, which is often affected by years of severe drought. In 1970, they decided to leave their families in the village and join the exodus to São Paulo, in search of jobs and a better life.

With 50 others, they made the long trek south on the back of a truck, hanging on to the *pau de arara*—the "parrot's perch" formed by poles running along the sides. The first few days were rough going, over dirt tracks, but soon there were paved roads, and after two weeks the travelers entered the big city. Luís went to stay with a brother in São Bernardo, the auto-manufacturing sub-

urb; Teotista, who had no relatives to help him out, looked for work on a building site. Over the next 15 years, their lives diverged sharply.

Luís' brother found him a job in the car factory, where he became a skilled toolmaker; a couple of years after he arrived, he sent money north for his wife, Bernadette, and his two children to join him. They now have a third child and Bernadette works at the local kindergarten. The eldest child, Teresa, hopes to become a teacher, and the second, Airton, wants to be an engineer.

The family lives in São Bernardo in their own house, which Luís, like most working-class Brazilians, designed and built himself with the help of relatives and friends. Whenever there is cash for more materials, he adds an extra room or pushes out a wall. Luís has been laid off work occasionally, but never for more than a month or two, and the family has always managed to get by. They have a color television and own a second-hand car—a Volkswagen Beetle—and on Sundays they sometimes drive to the beach or go fishing. The miracle has brought success for Luís

and his family, and they are firmly on the ladder upward.

But fortune did not smile on Teotista, who has never progressed beyond being an unskilled laborer and has twice been injured at work on building sites, where nobody bothers with such things as safety helmets or boots. His wife, Eva, and six children migrated from the northeast to join him; four more children were born after Eva arrived. The family lives far out of town in a tiny tumbledown shack, built from old lengths of wood and flattened oil drums, the gaps plastered with mud, and a sheet of plastic held down with bricks for a roof. A filthy stream nearby serves as a sewer.

When he has a job, it costs Teotista one fourth of his daily wage just to travel to and from work in a jam-packed bus. These days, with civil construction at a much lower level than in the 1970s, he is often out of work. He drinks a lot and sometimes disappears for days on end. Eva has to struggle to bring up their children on what she can earn as a cleaning woman. The children are often ill: One caught polio in the north,

and both of his legs are paralyzed; another has twice been rushed to the hospital with pneumonia. All of them are undernourished. The oldest girl, Sandra, has become a prostitute, while Maurício, one of the older boys, has been tempted into petty crime, picking pockets in the city center.

Teotista and Eva once tried going back to the north, but life was even worse there, with no land to cultivate. They heard through the grapevine about Luís' good fortune and, still with a tiny seed of hope in their hearts, returned to São Paulo to start again.

The endurance of such families seems almost heroic, and Teotista's story is by no means unusual in Brazil. The mass of the people can apparently be pushed and asked to make sacrifices to a degree almost unthinkable in developed countries without provoking an explosion. This is largely because during the boom years of the 1970s the pace of change and the degree of material progress enjoyed by most Brazilians was so great and so concentrated that the majority still feel dazed by it. Even those who missed out have a rel-

69

3

ative or acquaintance who prospered. People who are not utterly ground down by misfortune continue to believe that if they keep trying, work hard and encourage their children to study, they will get good jobs and, in the end, their family will make progress.

Unfortunately, the better education of which Brazilians dream is rarely available. During the 1960s and 1970s, while it was pouring resources into the university system, which benefited a small fraction of the population, Brazil neglected its primary schools. Poor pay for teachers meant low professional standards. The inadequate teachers still fill the primary education system, and the quality of instruction is extremely low. Pupils often fail to reach the standard required at the end of the school year and are required to repeat a grade. Less than two thirds of those who complete the first grade go beyond the fourth grade, and less than a quarter of that group goes on to secondary education. Recently, the imbalance in the allocation of educational resources has been recognized, and much attention is focused on the plight of the primary schools. But it will certainly be many years before all the faults in the system can be remedied.

Even in those areas where the schools are good—Brasília has a better reputation than most other cities—educational attainments are not high because many children drop out of school to earn money. In families such as Teotista's, they become invaluable breadwinners at a tender age. A boy or girl may become a domestic servant or an office messenger, may load shoppers' bags in the supermarkets or try to sell something at intersections when cars stop for traffic lights. When all these

small sums are added up, there may be enough to feed and clothe the family, and perhaps to buy a small plot of land on which to build a home.

When even this existence proves impossible, there may be no alternative to the *favela*, or shantytown. São Paulo, Brazil's economic capital, had fewer than 40,000 shanty dwellers in 1970, but the 1980 census revealed a surge to nearly 400,000. By the mid-1980s, with a third of the work force unemployed, the figure had risen another 200,000.

A *favela* starts with an *invasão*, which is sometimes organized but is usually a spontaneous invasion by homeless families of unused land near the heart of a city. It may be a swampy spot or, perhaps, the side of a hill that is too steep to be developed with conventional buildings. Thousands of people cram themselves into a jumble of shacks made from packing cases, old corrugated-iron sheets and cardboard, often with one shanty leaning on the next for support. Frequently, a family of 10 or more will crowd into a one-room shack. The stink that comes from the unpaved alleyways between the houses is dreadful—in many places there are no sewers, and the only way human waste and garbage are disposed of is by a heavy downpour of rain.

In some *favelas* there is no water supply, so the inhabitants carry water they have taken from public fountains or fire hydrants to their houses in kerosene cans. Inevitably, the remarkable growth of *favelas* has brought a wave of disease and a troubling upswing in Brazil's infant mortality rate, which had dropped steadily since the 1940s. Of the children born in 1980 in São Paulo, 14 percent died before they reached their first birthday.

The *favela* dwellers sometimes obtain

3

In the Japanese quarter of São Paulo, a vendor offers *camarão grande*—giant shrimp fried in batter. More than 300,000 Japanese emigrated to Brazil in the first half of this century; most settled in São Paulo state, forming Japan's largest overseas community.

an electricity supply illegally from the national power company, while others hook themselves up to the supplies of neighboring houses to whom they pay a handsome premium for the privilege. Mail is often addressed to a nearby house with a permanent address, then redistributed from there by the *favela's* own unofficial postal service.

Many *favelas* have been cleared by municipal authorities and their inhabitants moved to subsidized housing or apartments on the outskirts of the city, but this solution is not popular because of the additional traveling expenses involved and a general dislike among city dwellers of being away from downtown. In cases where the inhabitants of a *favela* begin to feel they are not in imminent danger of being disposessed, or where they have managed to lease the land from its owner, they usually begin making improvements to their houses, which can end up reasonably comfortable. A strong sense of community usually develops. Small neighborhood shops spring up selling goods on extended credit—though at inflated prices, since the shop owners do not have access to wholesalers.

Many families, in keeping with their rural backgrounds, keep chickens and even pigs in their minuscule yards, perhaps bringing the animals indoors at night with the family. Some set up tiny businesses, repairing cars or making gewgaws for sale. With no unemployment benefit to fall back on, the rest survive by roaming the streets in search of wastepaper, bottles and scrap metal, by searching the garbage cans for food and by begging.

Under the stresses of poverty and bad living conditions, many families disintegrate. The most tragic aspect of the breakdown is the plight of the chil

dren. Of an estimated 6.2 million children in the region of São Paulo, 20 percent live in the streets, not so much orphaned as abandoned by parents so poverty-stricken that they can no longer support them. The main worry of the children is that they will be apprehended by the police and locked up in a FEBEM, the acronym of the Foundation for the Education and Benefit of Minors. Intended as asylums for abandoned children, FEBEM depots long ago gave up any attempt to live up to the intention of their title and have simply become desolate and vandalized institutions where a token percentage of the children can be kept off the streets for a few nights.

Many of the "sufferers of the street," as they are known, are addicted to sniffing glue to stifle pangs of hunger. Some support themselves by scavenging garbage; some eke out a living as shoe cleaners or street traders, and some are hired by shopkeepers as assistant security staff at half the legal wage. Others lead a life that revolves around gambling-machine arcades, prostitution and petty thievery.

Crime has become a serious problem in urban Brazil. Thousands of murders are reported each year in São Paulo and Rio; many more go unreported. Around a quarter of all homes in the largest cities are burglarized in any one year. Holdups have become almost commonplace on the bus route between Rio and São Paulo. Despite the presence of armed security guards protecting the banks, shops and apartment buildings, and heavy policing in the better parts of the cities, the middle class is extremely worried. High crime rates undoubtedly reflect the desperate straits of countless Brazilians; many of the urban gangsters are the abandoned children of yesterday.

Even a casual visitor to Brazil recognizes that the underprivileged portion of society contains a disproportionate number of dark-skinned people. Quantifying that impression is, however, fraught with difficulty, not least

3

because of the Brazilian spectrum of skin shades, with every color gradation represented. Since whites began interbreeding with the native Indians four centuries ago, and with the Negro slaves not very long after, it is hardly surprising that the blending has been thorough. On the beaches, on the streets, the majority of Brazilians seem to be a mixed race, any permutation of European, African and, to a lesser extent, Amerindian.

The picture does vary somewhat from region to region. In the *favelas* of the large cities one could imagine oneself in West Africa. In the far south, the features of the 20th-century European immigrants predominate, while in the north and northeast, there are still numerous people with a pronouncedly Amerindian physiognomy. But millions of Brazilians everywhere fall into one of the intermediate categories generously provided for in Brazilian Portuguese. Between *côr do carvão,* ("coal color," a dark Negroid type) and *moreno* ("toast color," with straight or wavy hair), words can be found to distinguish more than a dozen different kinds of physical characteristics.

At the time of Brazil's first census, taken in 1872, whites accounted for less than 40 percent of the population. Over the next half century, immigration from Europe, the Middle East and Japan considerably lightened the Brazilian people. The 1950 census, the last to seek racial origins, classified the population as 62 percent white, 11 percent black and 27 percent mixed blood. That census can only be a rough guide, since it required people to make their own judgement as to their color. Most objective observers would assess the proportion of pure whites as considerably less than 62 percent. But distinc-

tions between white and near-white are of little consequence in Brazil. The most important division is somewhere in the middle of the mixed-bloods, or mulattoes. The experience of the dark mulattoes in Brazilian society is essentially the same as that of the blacks, while light mulattoes can live lives similar to those of whites. The blacks, together with the dark mulattoes, make up about 30 percent of the population.

Most Brazilians insist that the experience of blacks and whites in their country differs only to the extent that the blacks are poorer. Brazilian orthodoxy acknowledges that the historical handicap of slavery has placed most blacks in the lowest classes, but it does not admit to any racial discrimination today. Brazilians proudly describe their nation as a racial democracy, a land where people of every shade have an equal opportunity for social advancement. Indeed, so convinced are they of the truth of their claim that any attempt to question it is met with incredulity and wounded pride.

The philosophy of many in Brazil is to encourage a process called *branqueamento*—literally, "whitening." The idea is that continued interbreeding between the races will eventually make it impossible to separate out those who have African origins. Immigration of whites, although on a very small scale nowadays, also contributes toward the whitening of the nation. For the individual black with ambitions, the Brazilians have a phrase: "Money whitens." It is widely held that as a black becomes wealthier or better educated, blackness counts for less. Brazilians, thus, often assert that there is no prejudice against blacks as such, but merely against their low socioeconomic position.

Several facts appear superficially to

Young children learn to count on their fingers at a village school in Amazonia. Primary education is free in Brazil, and theoretically compulsory, but trained teachers are so scarce in country areas that only 1 child in 7 completes elementary school.

3

support the belief that blacks are equal in Brazil. First of all, there is the fact that overt racial discrimination has long been outlawed. The 1946 constitution prohibited discrimination on grounds of color, and the ban was given legal teeth in 1951 with the passing of a law that specified penalties for race discrimination in public places. Then there are the crowds in the streets and on the beaches, where people of quite different hues mingle together and socialize happily. Case histories can be produced, moreover, to show that mixed blood has never been an absolute barrier to advancement. Recently, there have been the successes of Pelé, the black soccer player, and numerous pop musicians; and as far back as 1909, there was even a president of mixed blood, Nilo Peçanha.

Certainly the friendliness between the races in Brazil is unique in a country with a slave-owning history. Gilberto Freyre, while documenting the crucial division in society that slave ownership produced, recorded many mitigating factors in colonial society. He stressed the affectionate relations between masters and slaves, and the lack of prejudice against the miscegenation of races. In his view, the Portuguese harbored considerable respect for the Africans, both on account of having once been ruled themselves by Moors and because of their Catholic religion, which obliged them to see the slaves not as mere chattels but as creatures with souls that could be saved.

Freyre's widely respected views have contributed in large measure to the myth of Brazil as a multiracial society free from the problems of racism that beset other countries. And there is much truth in that picture. The easygoing tolerance that dates back to the colonial period, together with the legal framework of equality, has at least prevented the kind of bitter polarization of black and white that has occurred in other countries. Although the Indians have suffered deeply at the hands of those who came later, racial violence is otherwise unknown in Brazil. And, with no tangible grievance to unite them, Brazilian blacks have been slow to react against the subtler forms of discrimination that have persisted since the slave epoch.

In the 1950s, the blacks of Brazil could count themselves far better off than those of the southern United States, who were segregated in public places, banned from private white clubs, restaurants, shops and institutions of higher education and debarred from all but menial jobs. American blacks had to fight for their civil rights in the 1960s, and in doing so not only won political reforms but also changed the whole climate of society. No similar transformation of racial attitudes has taken place in Brazil. As a result, clear-sighted observers find evidence both of widespread racial prejudice in Brazil today and of many pressures on blacks and dark mulattoes to remain in subservient positions.

Jokes about the morals, intelligence, honesty and reliability of blacks are commonplace, for example, and black women are subtly denigrated. In Brazilian folklore, mulatto women are passionate and promiscuous—ideal mistresses but not suitable as wives.

In employment, blacks often have extreme difficulty reaching high positions. Until recently, black Brazilians, however suitably qualified, were not admitted to the diplomatic service or to the Brazilian navy, which considered itself the elite of the country's armed forces. There are still very few blacks at the upper levels of the administration, business and commerce; and a mere handful of the 548 members of the Brazilian Congress are black. The poverty of blacks cannot alone explain these low figures: The immigrants from Europe and Asia who have settled in Brazil over the past 100 years often possessed no more than the blacks during their early years, and they have succeeded in rising rapidly. The much-vaunted people of mixed race who do reach the top are far more often pale-skinned mulattoes than dark-complexioned blacks.

The job advertisements that appear in the large-city newspapers for shop assistants or clerical staff frequently specify *boa aparência*. Everyone in Brazil knows that this phrase can be translated as "white or pale-skinned" as well as its literal meaning of "good appearance." Blacks get the message and do not bother to apply.

The convention regarding *boa aparência* is typical of the situation in Brazil today. There are no overt instances of discrimination, because there is no need for them. The system was neatly satirized recently by Millôr Fernandes, a Rio cartoonist, with the epigram "there is no racism in Brazil: The blacks know their place."

The minority of blacks who do make progress up the social scale are generally reluctant to jeopardize their position by complaining about prejudice. Rather, they tend to understate their blackness, and many marry fairer-skinned people so their children will be paler. Nevertheless, Afro-Brazilian consciousness has been emerging.

The first organization to stand up for the rights of black people was the Brazilian Negro Front, which was founded in São Paulo in 1931. Committed to

The black worshipper in a Rio church and the idealized Caucasian portrayed on her shopping bag bear silent testimony to the social gulf between white and black. In spite of laws forbidding racial discrimination, most of Brazil's estimated 12 million blacks remain at the poorest levels of society.

nonviolence, it created a political party, organized political demonstrations and published a newspaper. In 1937, during the Vargas era, it was banned, along with other political organizations.

There was a revival of black conciousness in 1945 under Abdias do Nascimento, a playwright who is considered the father of the modern black rights movement in Brazil. Nascimento founded the Afro-Brazilian Democratic Committee; the committee, however, had little clout after the military coup of 1964. Despite the inspiration of the decolonization of Africa and the progress of the civil rights movement in the United States, black political awareness in Brazil subsided into a long period of quiescence. It was not dead, however. As successive military governments relaxed their authoritarianism, a group called the Unified Black Movement against Racial Discrimination brought 5,000 people out into the streets of São Paulo in 1978 to protest against an overt act of racism in a sports club. It was the first public demonstration against racism seen in Brazil for many years, and it heralded a heightened racial consciousness.

Since Brazil's return to democracy in 1985, many new groups promoting Afro-Brazilian cultural identity and protesting against various forms of discrimination have appeared. Most of them are nonmilitant. Only a tiny handful of blacks participate in such groups; but their influence is spreading. The number of black Brazilians who are proud of their color and prepared to insist on their rights is growing. Although Freyre's image of masters and slaves is still very relevant to the Brazilian social order, it may not be long before the slaves shake off their invisible shackles. □

COWBOYS OF THE PAMPAS

Photographs by Claus C. Meyer

For 200 years, the vast pampas of southern Brazil have been the trackless domain of cattle, horses and gauchos, the free-spirited cowboys who ride with the herds. Usually of mixed Portuguese and Indian ancestry, the first gauchos were true nomads of the grass-lands. They rode where they pleased, taming mustangs when they wanted fresh mounts. If they needed money, they killed the half-wild cows that roamed the pampas and sold the valuable hides, leaving the carcasses to rot in the sun.

Today, the cattle are branded, the pampas are fenced, and the gauchos are employees of ranchers and beef companies. Responsible for enormous herds of prize cattle, they ride for long days, driving animals from one thousand-acre pasture to another. They notch ears and brand haunches, nurse sick cows, dehorn calves and castrate young bulls. Today, their independent spirit is tethered by the rigorous work. Yet their knowledge of the pampas, their stamina and their superb horsemanship have not changed since the 19th century, when poems and ballads enshrined them as folk heroes.

On a roundup, several hundred head of cattle are herded through a gate. Shifting animals to fresh grazing land or driving them to the slaughterhouse may mean a week on the trail, with the gauchos sleeping under the stars, using their ponchos as groundsheets and their saddles as pillows.

Surrounded by *domadors*, the gaucho horse-breakers, a wild-eyed colt rears in terror as he feels the weight of the saddle for the first time. Although this moment is often frenzied, the horses are broken in gradually, with gentle handling over many months. The traditional saddle, constructed without a pommel or a cantle, is a sandwich of leather pads and wool blankets. A thick sheepskin lies on top to prevent saddle sores during long rides. The stirrups are a recent innovation: Gauchos once rode barefoot, gripping leather straps between their toes to keep their balance.

Gleaming with silver medallions and coins, a gaucho's wide leather belt is a treasured part of his gear and is often passed from father to son. The belt is buckled over a blue sash and a hide apron, worn to protect the legs.

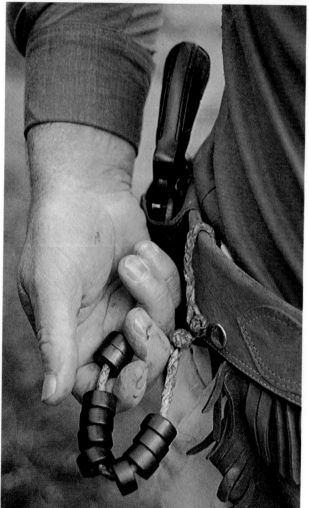

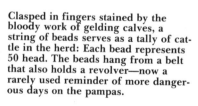

Clasped in fingers stained by the bloody work of gelding calves, a string of beads serves as a tally of cattle in the herd: Each bead represents 50 head. The beads hang from a belt that also holds a revolver—now a rarely used reminder of more dangerous days on the pampas.

On the steps of a vine-covered outbuilding, a gaucho punches new holes in his horse's bridle. The men are skilled harness makers, fashioning their own tack (*right*) from the grasslands' plentiful supply of cowhide.

Early on a rainy summer evening, the gauchos move their usual outdoor barbecue into the stable, where accordion music rises above the sizzle of roasting

meat. The menu is always the same: bitter herbal tea sipped from a gourd, and prime beef, seasoned with salt and grilled over the fire on a skewer.

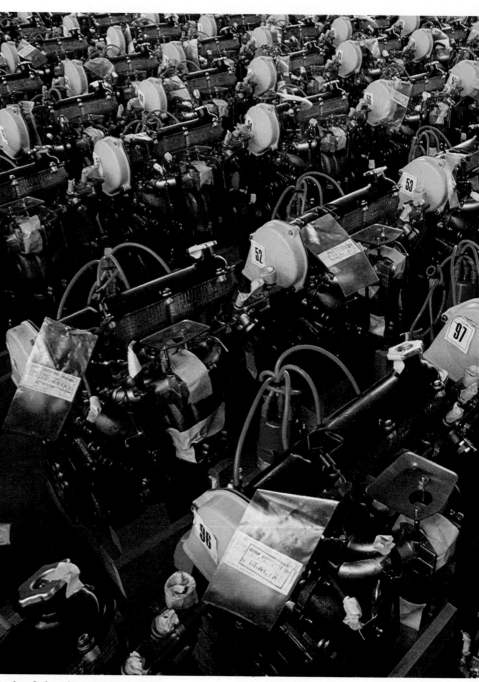

Ranks of gleaming new car engines await shipment to Italy from Fiat's giant factory at Belo Horizonte, capital of Minas Gerais. Fiat arrived in Brazil in 1974, soon after General Motors, Ford and Volkswagen, and by 1980, the "big four" were producing more than one million cars per year.

AN ECONOMIC ROLLER COASTER

It has been more than 400 years since the last foolhardy adventurer to sail up the Amazon in search of El Dorado vanished beneath the river's impassive surface. Yet the conviction that Brazil's vast hinterland offers riches beyond measure dies hard among the gamblers of the world, and in 1967, their number was swelled by Daniel K. Ludwig, an American multimillionaire and entrepreneur. Ludwig's El Dorado was made of paper, not gold: He planned to capture a large part of the world market in wood pulp. In the first phase of an ambitious $700-million scheme, he bought 3.7 million acres of Amazon forest along the Jari River and floated a complete pulp-making factory halfway around the globe from Japan. He then planted millions of saplings of what he believed to be the world's fastest-growing tree, the gmelina, a native of the rain forests of Asia.

To hedge his bet and so fully exploit the resources of his Jari property, Ludwig also planned the world's largest rice-paddy and the world's largest palm-tree plantation. A mixed farming operation would produce crops including sugar, corn, manioc and castor beans, while 50,000 head of cattle would graze on a massive ranch. Nor did Ludwig forget the riches beneath the soil: Gold, diamonds, tin and bauxite were the genies in the bottle that would finance the entire project.

By 1980, Jari had a work force of 7,000, with its own schools, hospitals, harbor and airport. But two years later, the Amazon claimed one more in a long line of victims. The cost of pulping had proved higher than anticipated; the super-trees had failed to grow fast enough or had simply died in the dry season; and the costs of mining and farming were astronomic. With losses mounting to $75 million, Ludwig, once reported to be the world's richest man, disposed of 40 percent of his dream to a Brazilian entrepreneur, and the remainder went to a consortium of bankers, financiers and construction companies, who then proceeded to scale down the project considerably. By the mid-1980s, the Jari project was just breaking even but was nowhere near paying off its fearsome debts.

Taken in isolation, the rise and fall of Ludwig's aspirations was only one in a long line of dreams of wealth that have been disappointed during the history of Brazil's development. Time and again, ignoring basic development, the nation has pinned all its economic hopes on a single export commodity, only to see the market collapse, leaving it to search desperately for an alternative. For 400 years, this narrow ambition has taken the entire country—leaders, speculators, citizens and slaves—on a desperate, unending roller-coaster ride of boom and bust. In the 1970s, Brazil reached the brink of glory when, after 20 years of astonishing growth, the nation appeared to be slipping through the eye of the economic needle to take its place among the major powers.

Brazil achieved its industrial transformation in a very short time. From the modest industrial base established by President Getúlio Vargas in the 1930s, Brazil made two great strides into industrialization: the first between 1947 and 1961, under a democratic government; the second between 1968 and 1974, under a military government. In the latter period alone the economy grew by 50 percent, and it reached a staggering 14 percent growth rate in 1973, the peak year. Growth continued more steadily until the end of the decade, when Brazil was able to claim that it had more than quadrupled its economy in size, from $45 billion to $205 billion. It was now the eighth-largest economy in the Western world and was in the top 10 for steel production, electricity generation, automobile manufacturing and ore mining. It also became the world's third-largest food producer, after the United States and France.

But in 1980, the boom ended with a resounding crash that left Brazil the world's largest debtor, owing 700 overseas banks a total of $100 billion—$833 for every man, woman and child in the country. In all but proportion, this spectacular collapse, which would have threatened the economy of the entire Western world had Brazil reneged on its debts, was no more than another familiar instance of economic failure in a whole series that have recurred throughout Brazil's history. In Brazil, it seems, the alternative to full-scale success is complete ruin.

Ever since the Portuguese colonized this vast territory in the 16th century, Brazil has exploited its resources one at a time, going from monoculture to monoculture. Whatever crop was likely to fetch a high price on the world's markets was planted on a large scale: Alternative crops were ignored, and the development of a solid base of mixed farming was neglected because it did not yield the high profits expected by Brazil's plantation owners. But the price of their short-sighted opportunism was a profound vulnerability to sudden shifts in international demand.

The first boom, built on sugar cane planted, reaped and milled by thousands of African slaves, started in the 17th century and went bust in the 18th century when slaves on Caribbean and North American plantations began to produce the crop more cheaply. The second, the gold rush in the state of Minas Gerais at the end of the 18th century, brought a shift in population from the north to the south of the country, but foundered a century later when the gold seams were exhausted. However, the profits from mining financed the third and longest-lasting boom: coffee. The beans were first planted in the 1790s in the state of Rio de Janeiro, and later around the worked-out gold fields of Minas Gerais. By 1845, almost half the nation's export earnings came from coffee, the continued growth of which stimulated another round of immigration: 800,000 new settlers arrived between 1870 and 1900, three quarters of them from Italy, the rest from Portugal, Germany and central Europe.

The age of coffee was punctuated briefly by a world demand for the natural rubber of Amazonia, at that time the only known source. The rubber boom began in the last quarter of the 19th century, after the pneumatic tire was invented, but it collapsed abruptly in 1913, undermined by Britain's Malayan plantations, themselves the result of rubber seeds from Brazilian stock. The speculators who had swarmed up the Amazon in the 1880s departed within three decades.

Luckily for the Brazilian economy, there was a growing demand for coffee, and production rose steadily to a peak of 28.5 million bags (each weighing 132 pounds) in 1930—about the level it remains today. At the same time, Brazil's coffee barons and investors from Britain and the United States were taking the first tentative steps toward building an elementary industrial infrastructure. The Brazilian government borrowed huge sums to build railroads and ports; gas and electricity were installed in some of the larger cities. So, when the worldwide Great Depression of 1929 triggered a collapse in the price of coffee, the familiar elements of a Brazilian economic crisis were all neatly in place: a large foreign debt and total dependence on a single crop.

Now, at last, the solution to the country's recurring economic problems began to dawn on the government and Brazil's financial elite: The hair-raising cycle of boom and bust would never be broken until Brazil could diversify its agricultural production and build a manufacturing industry strong enough to ride out setbacks in any one sector of the economy. Moreover, Brazil also had to create a domestic market large enough to maintain a minimum demand for its goods during periods of recession. To create a sound industrial base, the country would need additional investment, funded by still more borrowing from abroad; to develop a market, Brazil would need a well-paid work force with cash to spend. The trouble was that 90 percent of Brazil's population, 42 million people at the beginning of World War II, were unpaid peons

working on plantations in conditions little better than slavery, or they were peasants trying to scratch a subsistence living from the country's least productive land.

The rush for industrial growth began in earnest under Getúlio Vargas, who seized power in October 1930 and ruled Brazil almost without interruption until 1956. Modeling himself to some extent on Italy's Benito Mussolini and ruling by decree, Vargas established state-controlled, and therefore pliable, labor unions and plowed state capital into cornerstone enterprises, such as the country's first steel mill, which opened at Volta Redonda in 1946, as well as a National Develop-

ment Bank and the oil-refining monopoly Petrobras, both inaugurated in the early 1950s.

Vargas' contribution to Brazil's development as an industrial nation was considerable, but he was building on a very low base, and when he left office in 1956, much remained to be done to unlock the massive resources of the country's interior. One of the main weaknesses was communications: The railroads could hardly be described as a system, much less a network, connecting, as they did, only a few scattered areas inland from the main ports. Roads were rudimentary, usually little more than unpaved tracks vulnerable to the weather. Inland journeys could

take on epic proportions during the rainy season, when fords became impassable and flimsy bridges built out of tree trunks were swept away. Passengers on buses would prepare themselves with food and clothing for journeys that could take weeks, during which they often had to disembark and help dig out a vehicle buried in mud. It was not uncommon for truck drivers to carry guns so that, if they were stranded on the road, they could go hunting for wild game to supplement their provisions. It was much easier to travel by ship than by road from Belém or Recife, in the northeast, to Rio or São Paulo, in the central south.

When Vargas' successor as president,

4

Juscelino Kubitschek, came to power in 1956, he immediately turned his attention to Brazil's communications problems. As governor of the state of Minas Gerais during the Vargas years, he had given priority to hydroelectric power and road building, and as national leader, he extended that priority right across the country. The keystone of his plan was to move the capital from Rio de Janeiro, on the coast, to a place closer to the center of the country—a bare tract of scrubland in the state of Goiás. It was to be the focal point of a huge network of roads that would unite Brazil's distant frontiers and integrate its development as an industrial nation.

Kubitschek also commissioned the 1,000-mile-long Belém-Brasília Highway, much of it hacked clear across the Amazon forest to provide the country's first year-round route to the north. In addition, he took the first steps toward establishing a mass consumer industry. With new roads, there was new demand for motor vehicles: Vargas encouraged a local auto industry to expand production, and soon Ford, General Motors, Volkswagen and Fiat were among the biggest employers. The populations of the cities swelled enormously as peasants from the rural northeast left the land in droves, heading south to find jobs in construction or in the new industries that were springing up in the so-called ABCD suburbs of São Paulo—Santo André, São Bernardo, São Caetano and Diadema.

The price of Kubitschek's achievement, however, was a massive increase in borrowing from abroad and rampant inflation—problems that were inherited by the presidents of the two short-lived governments that followed. Both presidents found themselves caught between the conflicting wishes of Brazil's international creditors, who wanted to see a more realistic approach to the management of the Brazilian economy, and the growing class of industrial workers, who objected increasingly vociferously to the implied squeeze on wages and living standards.

The first of Kubitschek's successors, Jânio Quadros, tried to please the bankers and the International Monetary Fund, and his government fell after less than a year in office. The second, João Goulart, a left-wing populist, tried to appease the trade unions, and inflation soared. In 1964, labor unions, middle-class radicals in the cities and left-wing peasant leagues were becoming more vocal in their demands for political and agrarian reform. There were demonstrations and mutinies in the armed forces, and the economy showed signs of faltering. On April 1, 1964, a group of army generals, convinced that the country had become ungovernable and that the leftward swing of politics had gone far enough, took control of Brazil.

The austerity of the first period of military government soon gave way to repression as strikes were all but outlawed and union leaders were thrown into prison. There was no more collective bargaining: The state, not the managements and the labor unions, decided what pay increases would be given. Increases were announced just once a year: an austerity measure in itself when inflation was running at 80 percent. At the same time, credit was severely controlled, which resulted in a decrease in domestic demand; tax collection was tightened up; and wage-price indexing was introduced—a mechanism that linked all prices and costs to the rate of inflation. As the inflation rate fell from 80 percent to 25 percent in just two years, so wage hikes, rents, public service charges and transportation costs all fell in turn.

Yet the military had no intention of abandoning growth as a goal. If anything, their vision of Brazil's future was the most grandiose ever: to make Brazil a front-ranking world power by the year 2000, negotiating on equal terms with the United States, Western Europe and Japan. They appointed Antônio Delfim Netto, a technocrat who had achieved a brilliant reputation as professor of economics at the University of São Paulo, to usher in "the decade of the miracle." A born optimist and bon vivant, Delfim had an expansive personality to match his substantial girth and brought his exuberance into national affairs. A group of economists, known as "Delfim's boys," soon took up key positions in the power network.

The dynamic Delfim was quick to realize that conditions were extremely favorable to tempt foreign capital into Brazil. Throughout the industrial world, corporations were beset by the soaring costs of labor, energy and materials. Brazil could offer large companies all three commodities at competitive rates, as well as a domestic market that was estimated to reach 30 million wage earners by the year 1985. All that the country needed was capital; and this the foreign companies could supply themselves, or local firms could borrow from abroad.

The economy boomed, giving plenty of scope for Brazilians to profit. For the rich, there were constant opportunities for investment and reinvestment in industry, and the profits were handsome—because capital gains were (and still are) untaxed. As the cities expanded, everyone who was anyone bought a second or third weekend house on the coast or in the mountains near the cities; fortunes were made from buying and selling land and in property development. Cement production, spurred on by the construction bonanza, grew between 1970 and 1980 from nine million tons to 27 million tons. Industry increased its output by 233 percent between 1970 and 1979, commerce by 211 percent and transportation by 215 percent. The auto industry more than tripled production from 416,000 vehicles in 1970 to 1.6 million in 1980, while the output of trucks shot from fewer than one million a year in 1970 to almost three million in 1980. At the same time, a spectacular road-building program was initiated, drawing the farthest corners of the country closer together, including the 3,480-mile Trans-Amazonian Highway, which was carved through virgin forest all the way across Brazil from east to west. The only laggard was agriculture, which registered a relatively modest 156 percent increase during the decade.

On that kind of economic growth, Brazil became the world bankers' favorite investment prospect. Loan money poured into the country from abroad despite several cautionary signals that lenders somehow failed to heed. The first was the world oil crisis of 1973, when the price of crude oil skyrocketed—from two dollars a barrel to more than $12, pushing up the price of goods in the industrialized nations and doubling Brazil's import bill. At the same time, commodity prices plunged, which brought down the value of Brazil's exports. But by that time there was a glut of money entering the world's banking system from the Middle Eastern countries, now fabulously rich from their oil sales. The money had to be put to use somewhere, and with Eu-

Shielded from the sunlight by a blue plastic canopy, thousands of tender coffee seedlings flourish in the red soil of Paraná. One tenth of all Brazilians earn their living from coffee and the nation is by far the world's largest producer, growing more than 30 percent of the total harvest.

91

rope and the United States deep in recession, Brazil was one of the best investment prospects in the world.

In 1974, General Ernesto Geisel, an austere and authoritarian soldier, became president. But the blueprint for development scarcely changed: The national plan announced that year gave an additional boost to steel, chemical and nonferrous-metal production, as well as new investment in railways to carry increased tonnages of ores and processed metals. A contract was signed with West Germany for eight nuclear power stations, complete with fuel-processing plants. The estimated cost of the project, the biggest export order Germany had ever had, was $18 billion, but with interest payments on borrowing from international banks to pay for the project, the final figure Brazil would have to pay was estimated at closer to $30 billion.

A few skeptical voices from the political left, the universities and independent research centers warned that the economy had become dangerously overheated, but they were shrugged off by the military leadership. Then, as international interest rates began to climb, new borrowing was required just to keep pace with loan-maintenance commitments, and in 1975, the government was forced to put the first cautious controls on foreign loans. Aimed mainly at dampening the foreign borrowing of importers, these measures mainly affected the private sector: The state monopolies in energy production, minerals and transportation, which all had a large number of uncompleted development projects, continued to borrow unhindered. In 1972, two thirds of foreign loans had been made to private industry; only seven years later, however, two thirds of all new borrowing was done by the state.

The crunch came in 1979 when, as a result of the second world oil crisis, Brazil's import bill was pushed up once again, this time by four billion dollars, creating a trade deficit of three billion, and an overall deficit, including loans, of $15 billion. When Brazil requested more cash to service the debt, overseas bankers belatedly discovered in the small print of their house rules such restrictions as "country limits"—the maximum proportion of their total lending that could be made to any one country. The foreign bankers refused to extend any additional credit, and Brazil found itself teetering on the verge of bankruptcy.

The crash hit the pockets and the jobs of ordinary Brazilians with bewildering speed, and the political consequences were quick to follow. The greatest blow, however, was to Brazilian pride. Everything had seemed to be going so well: The country was trading with an ever-widening number of nations, and its international political clout was growing. In a decade of growth, the paid work force had doubled to 14.3 million people, incomes for nearly everyone in employment had risen, and the "trickle down" effect of spreading wealth was just beginning to improve the conditions of the masses of Brazilians living in poverty. Now Brazil was forced to go,

hat in hand, to the International Monetary Fund, admit that it had failed to run its own economy properly and ask for assistance.

The IMF's conditions were tough and followed the classic formula for restoring economies to health: Cut imports, increase exports and slash domestic consumption. Many Brazilians were outraged. Such a solution, they argued, might be suitable to a developed nation, but for a country like theirs, poised on the threshold of the First World, it was ruinous; what was needed was further growth to expand the domestic market and bring more people into the economy. In addition, with Brazil's ever-increasing population, 1.5 million jobs had to be created each year just to maintain the current level of unemployment. In the highest circles of government and finance, there was talk of Brazil declaring a unilateral moratorium on its debts, ignoring the international bankers, and working out its own economic salvation in isolation.

In the event, more sober counsel prevailed, and Brazil accepted the IMF's conditions. The *cruzeiro* was devalued by almost one third, wages were squeezed and the prices of essentials—such as fuel oil, electricity, gas, transportation and postal services—were raised. Food subsidies, earlier introduced to help the poor with mounting inflation, were phased out. As the chill wind of parsimony blew into every corner of the Brazilian economy, industry and commerce had to endure considerable belt-tightening.

In 1981, and again in 1983, the economy actually shrank, with industrial production declining by at least one fifth, and unemployment and underemployment standing at over 30 per-

cent of the work force. In São Paulo, "the locomotive that pulls the rest of Brazil," the Federation of Industries stated in 1983 that its member industries had reduced their manpower by 40 percent in the last couple of years, and that there were now only as many industrial workers in the state as there had been a decade previously. The civil construction industry, one of the most important employment opportunities for migrants to the cities, employed only half as many workers in 1983 as it had done a decade before. And for those who were out of work, there were no unemployment benefits to tide them over the difficult times.

By 1984, wages had fallen to the level of seven years earlier and matters were made even worse by inflation, which, during the first half of the 1980s, usually exceeded 100 percent and often peaked at more than 200 percent. During this period, the numbers of people living in *favelas* in places like São Paulo doubled, as new immigrants to the cities failed to find work and industrial workers lost their jobs. The middle classes, too, were by no means exempt from hardship, and their standard of living tumbled.

Cracks in the fabric of urban society began to appear in 1983 when crime increased sharply. That year the 2,840 murders reported in São Paulo alone made it one of the world's most violent cities. Burglary also reached epidemic proportions, but the most alarming development came in April 1983, when hundreds of supermarkets in cities all over Brazil were sacked and looted by rampaging mobs, whose main motive was simple hunger.

This was the first clear warning to the military government that time was running out. The patience of the mass es could no longer be taken for granted. For nearly two decades, the Brazilian working class had been remarkable for its political passivity: Indeed, this had been one of the aspects of the Brazilian economy that had attracted foreign investors. Much of this apparent stoicism about poor wages and working conditions had grown out of the optimism of the "miracle decade"—when industrial workers felt that, if they kept on trying and working hard at their jobs, they would progress up the ladder. Now the miracle was over, the hope was gone, and the sacrifices they were being asked to make seemed much less reasonable.

Popular pressure for the economic pie to be cut into fair shares mounted as the pie itself shrank. At the end of 1984, a flurry of industrial protest led by the embryonic left-wing PT, the Workers' party, signaled the end of the era of docile labor unions that had been inaugurated by Vargas in the 1930s. A new breed of leaders was emerging, encouraged by the example of the charismatic Luiz Inácio da Silva—better known as Lula.

One of hundreds of thousands of peasants who had made the trek down from the northeast on the back of an open truck, Lula was a fiery and accomplished public speaker who seemed instinctively to express the fears and aspirations of his fellow workers. Described by one of his opponents as "a force of nature," he had first made his mark as president of the São Bernardo Metalworkers' Union, whose 42-day strike in 1980, for a 15 percent wage increase, had taken the employers and the government utterly by surprise. Troops were sent in, Lula and 16 other leaders were arrested, and Lula was subsequently sacked from the union

MANAUS' MAGNIFICENT FOLLY

In a town surrounded by rain forest 1,000 miles up the Amazon stands one of the world's grandest opera houses—a fantastic relic of the rubber boom that shook this sleepy river port into vigorous life between 1880 and 1913. The huge profits made from Brazilian latex produced an instant plutocracy of rubber barons, who demanded the trappings of European luxury.

Manaus soon boasted public gardens, billiard rooms, a race track and a bull ring, but the town's crowning extravagance was its opera house, the Teatro Amazonas. The finest artists and artisans of Europe supplied its elegant fittings: paintings from Rome, chandeliers from Venice, roof tiles from Alsace, wrought iron from Glasgow, were shipped up the Amazon to Manaus.

On opening night in 1896, some 1,600 patrons sat beneath the pink cherubs cavorting on the theater ceiling. The gentlemen wore suits cleaned and pressed in Lisbon; the ladies sparkled with diamonds, for during the boom, more gems were sold in Manaus than anywhere else in the world.

Yet no full-length opera was ever staged at the Teatro Amazonas. Some stars of international caliber were lured by huge fees, but few performers were persuaded to risk the dangerous journey through the rain forest.

In 1913, when plantations in Southeast Asia began producing latex, Manaus' boom collapsed. The rubber barons were ruined and the opera house was closed. But since 1967, when the port was declared a duty-free zone, commerce has revived, renewing hope that the house will at last be put to its intended use.

Art nouveau chandeliers light the foyer of the theater, which was renovated in 1974.

Lovingly restored but rarely used, the imposing Manaus Opera House overlooks the Praça São Sebastião, paved in a traditional mosaic. A 19th-century monument commemorates the opening of Manaus to foreign shipping in 1868, when the Amazon port was little more than a village.

An allegorical painting of river-gods decorates the drop curtain used between acts.

4

leadership. Although charges of inciting an illegal strike hung over him for several years, Lula still succeeded in forming the PT, a radical political group that had spread all over the country and that, by 1984, was attracting support not only from industrial workers but also from rural people and middle-class radicals.

The military government was now convinced that its economic strategy was failing and that the attempt to meet the terms laid down by the IMF was impossible to sustain. For 21 years, it had governed in relative peace on the promise of achieving economic progress, but now there was real danger of a complete breakdown in law and order, if not of revolution; and the military no longer had the will to crush dissent, or even to rule. In the spring of 1985, a civilian administration prepared to take over, with Tancredo Neves, the president-elect, promising growth, prosperity and an end to the slump. It was a promise that clearly contained a veiled threat of refinancing Brazil's massive international debt, or even of declaring an indefinite moratorium on repayments. "Brazil's debt cannot be paid with people's hunger," declared the ailing Neves, who died before taking office. And his successor, President José Sarney, echoed the same defiant message.

The restoration of democracy in March 1985 was greeted by a wave of popular enthusiasm and relief throughout Brazil. Democracy was the theme of Carnival in several cities, and even the untimely death of Tancredo Neves, upon whom most Brazilians had pinned their hopes, could not dampen the revived spirit of national optimism that had swept the country. As far as the new government was concerned, this mood at least removed the pressing problem of rumbling revolt and social breakdown that had brought down its predecessors. Another breathing space came from the IMF, which gave the government time to take stock and come up with a solution to the problem of Brazil's international indebtedness.

In fact, the military government's balance sheet of economic achievement was by no means all bad, nor had the progress of the miracle decade been wasted. It had been the generals who, soon after assuming power in 1964, had taken the first steps toward integrating the external and internal sectors of the economy through the creation of official agencies to stimulate the development of the more backward regions. SUDECO (Superintendência do Desenvolvimento da Região Centro) and SUDESUL (Superintendência do Desenvolvimento da Região Sul) were set up to concentrate on the central west and the south; SUDENE and SUDAM had the more difficult task of the northeast and the Amazon. Success, however, had been patchy. In the backward northeast, where one quarter of Brazil's population live, SUDENE had created little new employment, and in 1985, almost half the population there still earned less than $100 a month: a negligible amount when required for the support of an average family with six children. In Amazonia, SUDAM was criticized for its support of large ranching operations and settlement programs that had subsequently failed, but it did earn applause for backing large-scale new mineral projects.

In general, however, the development boards were prime examples of a massive state bureaucracy that grew up under the generals—a bureaucracy whose corruption, incompetence and ostentation became a national byword. Despite the appointment of a minister of debureaucratization, the state sector had become so bloated by the mid-1980s that it was running no fewer than 550-odd state enterprises; all together, these agencies accounted for more than half the country's economy.

The continuing emphasis on the public sector—curious, to say the least, under a regime committed to free-enterprise capitalism—was very apparent. Unlike the United States or Europe, where the headquarters of major private companies are invariably vast, luxuriously appointed and far more prominent than those of public bodies, the prime sites in Brazil's cities were occupied by the headquarters of dozens of state corporations, which had their buildings designed by the country's best architects, had the largest and most conspicuous offices, and the brightest, most attractive and best-dressed staffs.

In Rio de Janeiro, a trio of three massive office buildings—the offices of the National Development Bank, the National Housing Bank, and Petrobras, the state-owned oil company—stood grouped together in splendid isolation on prime real estate. In the capital, Brasília, the most lavish building of all was the Central Bank, a soaring, elegant tower of tinted glass, its sheer heights broken by hanging gardens. Ministers and top officials lived like tycoons, occupying palatial residences along the lakeside and vying with one another for the largest number of domestic workers and the biggest swimming pools. The highest in the pecking order had their own jets, or they called on the Air Force to whisk them from one end of the country to the other.

In a campaign to cut oil imports, a poster urges Brazilians to fuel their cars with alcohol distilled from sugar cane. The sign carries two warnings: Do not mix with gasoline; do not use in unconverted engines. More than 40 percent of Brazil's cars use alcohol.

Inevitably, bureaucratic disregard for the finer points of commercial viability, combined with the generals' grandiose vision of Brazil's future, had resulted in some expensive white elephants. The nuclear development program, which had cost $2.5 billion by 1985, had ground to a halt, with only two of the contracted eight power stations likely to be completed. A "Steel Line" railroad, planned to link the iron-ore mines of Minas Gerais with the steel mills of São Paulo, Rio de Janeiro and the ports, had been abandoned after two billion dollars had been spent on preparing the rail bed and blasting through the mountains. After the unfinished line had been allowed to fall into disrepair, it was found that existing lines could cope quite easily with the volume of traffic. Many people also doubted that the $131 million spent on the Trans-Amazonian Highway could ever be justified: Not only were sections of it continually being washed away in tropical rainstorms, but it also ran parallel to the Amazon River, a natural transportation artery.

One of the military government's greatest mistakes had been in failing to develop agriculture in step with industry. During the miracle decade, there had been a 13 percent rise in the output of crops for export, but only a 1.7 percent increase in domestic food production. After two decades of considerable growth in population, the amount of food—including staples such as corn, beans, rice and manioc—that was available for each Brazilian had declined by one fifth. The problem the generals had failed to address was the oldest in Brazilian economic history: an excessive emphasis on growing cash crops for export at the expense of developing a broadly based agricultural economy.

During the years of military rule, the new fashionable crop of Brazil's agribusiness was soybeans. In 14 years, soybean production increased eightfold, until it reached 16 million tons in 1984 and earned three billion dollars in exports, mainly to the United States. But by 1985, the basic law of supply and

4

demand sent prices tumbling, and it seemed that soybeans would be joining the long list of export crops that have gone bust in Brazil. In the meantime, domestic food production languished, remaining disproportionately concentrated in the south, where a relatively small number of farmers descended from European immigrants, and with a European tradition of mixed farming, were settled.

Another major agricultural challenge that the military government had failed to confront was inequality of land distribution—a problem that owed its origins to the 17th century and the plantation families who spent much of their energies in consolidating huge landholdings. In the 1980s, half the country's best arable land was still in the hands of less than 1 percent of the landowners, and their huge plantations, which were sometimes underused or not cultivated at all, provided the barest income for a vast army of some nine million landless agricultural laborers. Another 9 percent of farmers had one third of the land, and the remaining 90 percent, usually subsistence peasants, owned less than one fifth.

For President Sarney's democratic government, the long-term agricultural prospects looked very bleak. Turning the millions of landless laborers into skilled farmers was itself a daunting task. And when the government announced a program of land redistribution to peasant settlers, the plantation landowners reacted in fury. Although the land-reform proposal offered generous compensation for any land to be expropriated, the landowners wanted none of it, and they were one of Brazil's most powerful lobbies; so formidable was this lobby that even the military government, which had also recog-

nized the urgency of land reform, had balked at confronting it.

The most valuable legacy of 21 years of military rule was the substantial improvement that had been made to the country's infrastructure. The improvement had been financed primarily by borrowing from abroad, but most people feel that the country's $108-billion foreign debt was well spent. The Trans-Amazonian Highway may have been a disappointment; but elsewhere, a road network reaches the remotest corners of Brazil's interior, and great strides were made in harnessing the country's hydroelectric potential, calculated as the fourth-largest in the world.

In 1984, the first of 18 massive turbines started to turn at the $18-billion Itaipu Dam—the world's largest—on the Paraná River, which marks the border of Paraguay and Brazil. Itaipu is intended to generate enough power to satisfy the projected industrial needs of São Paulo and Rio de Janeiro until the end of the century. The Tucurui Dam in Amazonia is equally impressive, holding back the Tocantins River, a tributary of the Amazon, with one of the longest barriers ever built. Opened in 1984, the Tucurui Dam is designed to power the nearby Carajás mining complex, which boasts one of the world's largest deposits of iron ore, as well as significant amounts of aluminum and other metals.

These two giant projects are a key element in opening the way to the development of Brazil's massive and still largely untapped mineral wealth. For many years, geologists have guessed at their existence, but Brazil still lags far behind other mineral-producing countries in accurately mapping its underground riches. This is partly because extreme tropical weather conditions

This hillside at Carajás, in the Amazonian forest, conceals the world's largest iron mountain, discovered in 1967 when a geologist was forced to land his helicopter on the top. Carajás has reserves of more than 18 billion tons of iron ore, and large deposits of bauxite, manganese and copper.

have leached the land of telltale surface traces of minerals, but also many of them are hidden beneath the impenetrable rain-forest canopy. In addition, mining has proved uneconomic on account of the lack of infrastructure, the expense of importing skilled labor, and the distance from the markets.

Until fairly recently, these difficulties have deterred international mining companies from exploiting Brazil's riches. However, spurred on by the discovery of Carajás' iron ore and bauxite, many companies have been quietly expanding their prospecting programs, and it is now thought that Brazil has huge deposits of nearly all commercially mined minerals—the exceptions appear to be metals in the platinum group, cobalt and vanadium.

The availability of cheap electricity, which is crucial to the smelting process, has given additional impetus to mineral extraction, and in 1984, Brazil surpassed Australia as the world's largest iron-ore exporter. Development of the country's huge bauxite resources is also now going rapidly ahead: A Brazilian-Japanese consortium and an Anglo-American company have started separate smelting plants in Amazonia, which are expected to be producing between them a total of one million tons of aluminum annually before the end of the 1980s. In addition, Brazil is also looking for ways of profiting from its proven reserves of 300,000 tons of uranium—one of the largest known deposits in the world—most of which were discovered after the initiation of Brazil's ill-fated nuclear power program.

Not all of Brazil's minerals are being extracted and processed by big companies. In Amazonia, where gold is usually found in small, isolated alluvial deposits, and where the difficulties of the

terrain often make large-scale mining impossible, an army of half a million independent diggers are searching for gold through the mud and sand of hundreds of hillsides and rivers. Many die from tropical diseases, in accidents, and in fights with rivals or Indians who object to the prospectors' encroachment on their territories. But as a result of their efforts, Brazil's output of gold rose dramatically from about five tons a year in 1979 to more than 50 tons in 1985. If the world gold price stays high enough to make it worthwhile for the prospectors, the country's gold output could reach between 70 and 100 tons annually, which would rank Brazil as the world's second-largest gold producer, behind South Africa.

Brazil's most superlative achievement has been to go most of the way toward solving its oil problems. It was the 1979 world oil price rise that had caused the country's financial crisis by pushing its import bill beyond an acceptable point; in 1981, the country was still spending a huge $10.5 billion on imported oil, a sum that nearly wiped out its export earnings, but the search had already started for alternative sources of fuel, and for oil itself.

At first, oil exploration, spread out along Brazil's Atlantic seaboard, yielded significant but not spectacular amounts. In 1982, however, a field called the Campos Basin, situated between 50 and 75 miles offshore from Rio de Janeiro, began delivering oil and gas; by 1985, production topped 600,000 barrels a day, lifting Brazil to third position among the Latin American oil producers, after Mexico and Venezuela. At the same time, an even richer field was located in the Campos Basin, and although it was 2,625 feet under the sea—a depth never tackled

before—Petrobras succeeded in sinking a well. Brazilians were confidently predicting that oil supplies, together with other existing fuel sources, would be sufficient to meet the country's requirements by 1990.

But even the oil discoveries would not have given Brazil this promise without the contribution of a remarkable effort by the government to reduce the country's dependence on mineral fuel and find alternative sources of energy. Prodded by officials, many companies switched from oil to electricity, and even to organic fuels such as wood charcoal and sugar-cane waste. The unexpected star of the alternate-energy plan, however, was found in the form of alcohol distilled from humble sugar.

In 1984, more than 2.4 billion gallons of alcohol were produced from sugar cane, supplying 4 percent of the country's total energy needs, and by the late 1980s, more than 90 percent of all new cars sold in Brazil were fitted with engines that run on the fuel. The sugar plantation owners, with the help of large government subsidies, tripled the amount of land devoted to the crop in a decade, and the alcohol program replaced 120,000 barrels of oil a day and sliced more than one billion dollars off the annual import bill.

Despite such victories on the import side, Brazil must achieve equal success in expanding its exports if it is to meet the conditions laid down by the IMF. Since 1982, the country has managed a healthy and increasing surplus of exports over imports. The export drive has been spearheaded in many cases by immigrants who moved to Brazil after World War II. Industries lacking detailed knowledge of a particular part of the world find a pool of energetic salespeople with international contacts,

In the duty-free port of Manaus, youngsters tempt tourists with trays of cheap goods, varying from socks and belts to Christmas decorations. Millions of poor Brazilian families depend on the meager profits their children make from such trading.

ready and willing to search for orders anywhere and everywhere.

One typical example is Nunzio Qaratem. Back in the early 1970s, when Brazil had a large chicken-breeding industry for domestic markets but no export market, he toured his native Middle East looking for customers. At first he got nowhere: Dealers had never heard of Brazilian chicken and were reluctant to take risks. In desperation, Qaratem stretched the truth and told dealers in Abu Dhabi that he had a very good order from Iraq, which would enable him to offer them a special low rate, and so wheedled from them a trial order for 200 tons.

To get the chickens to his customers, Qaratem had to persuade the state shipping company, Lloyd Brasileiro, to reroute a ship, at great expense, to Abu Dhabi. But the effort paid off: In 1984, Brazil exported 250,000 tons of frozen chicken, 90 percent of it to the Middle East, and earned $300 million. Nunzio Qaratem became a wealthy man and president of the Brazilian Association of Chicken Exporters.

Brazil's drive to export has benefited from the policy started during the military rule of shifting the country's production away from basic commodities—coffee, sugar, cocoa, cotton, iron ore and tobacco—toward manufactured and processed goods. By 1981, manufactured goods represented 62 percent of Brazil's total exports. In the late 1980s, most exports were factory-made goods, such as textiles, paper, vehicles, steel, shoes and a wide range of consumer goods, as well as such sophisticated manufactures as aircraft, armaments and computers.

It is on the development of an advanced technological base that Brazil has pinned its hopes for the future, and its aviation and armaments industries, built up at immense initial cost, are now mounting a challenge to more advanced industrial nations. The Empresa Brasileira de Aeronáutica (EMBRAER) was set up in 1970, when the government decided it could no longer afford to import the huge number of

4

light planes demanded by its farmers and businessmen. Financed jointly by the government and private investors, the industry first concentrated on building light aircraft such as the Ipanema, which was designed for agricultural use. EMBRAER's first export success was the Bandeirante 18- to 20-seat passenger plane, which came on the market in 1971. By the late 1980s, more than 400 Bandeirantes had been sold; the United States became an important export market once the plane had won its struggle for a certificate of airworthiness, granted against fierce opposition from North American manufacturers. EMBRAER then developed the two-seater Tucano trainer plane, named after the colorful Amazonian bird, which won a great marketing breakthrough when Britain's Royal Air Force ordered more than 130 in 1985. With a line of 12 aircraft, EMBRAER is now the sixth-largest aircraft manufacturer in the world.

Although Brazil has had a relatively low military expenditure for years because it has avoided an arms race with its neighbors, the military government started to develop armored cars about 15 years ago. Two versions of these, the Urutu and the Cascavel, named after poisonous snakes, are now used by the Brazilian armed forces and have also been sold to several Arab nations, who find them rugged, simple in design and easy to maintain. Brazil's fearsome Astro rocket launchers, capable of raining tons of Brazilian-made rockets on a small target several miles away, have also been supplied to the Iraqi army. The arms industry now earns an estimated three billion dollars in export sales each year.

The automobile manufacturing industry has also expanded since the 1980 financial crisis. Attracted to Brazil by the cheapness of labor, the "big four" multinational auto manufacturers have invested $500 million equipping factories to make the latest model world cars for sale around the globe: Brazilian-made Ford Escorts are cheaper in Scandinavia today than those made in Spain or Britain; General Motors ships hundreds of thousands of engines to its plants around the world; Volkswagen is planning to sell in the United States; and Fiat is exporting cars to Italy.

By 1984, the sacrifices of Brazil's wage earners and the efforts of its manufacturing and mining industries were beginning to pay off. The import bill had been cut by 15 percent in 1981, by 12 percent in 1982 and by a huge 23 percent in 1983. In 1984, exports increased by 23 percent, creating a record trade surplus of $12 billion—and a surge of optimism about the future. Observers in the late 1980s predicted that, with the heavy industrial base completed, scarcely any new borrowing would be needed for at least a decade, and much of what was owed abroad could be repaid.

The steel industry, for example, more than doubled its output from 8.4 million tons in 1975 to 18.7 million tons in 1984, becoming the world's eighth largest and one of the most modern. It is now saving Brazil a fortune every year: The cost of importing steel shrank from one billion dollars to only $138 million in 1984. Over that same period, steel exports earned almost nine billion dollars, approaching half the original $20-billion investment. Similar arguments apply to aluminum, tin, wood pulp and paper, shipbuilding and many other industries.

But there are pessimists who find equal cause for gloom. The record exports of 1984 will not be repeated, they claim, because barriers against Brazilian imports are now being raised in the United States, formerly the country's largest market. Competitors there, as in Western Europe, see Brazil as a threat, encroaching on their own overseas markets and domestic industries. Although the Western nations are anxious for Brazil to pay its debts, they also fear the emergence of another Japan, which would rock the economic boat and cause them more unemployment and social problems. The pessimists predict that, until the end of the century, the country will be stuck fast on a treadmill, struggling to pay off its creditors and making no progress at all—indeed, sliding inexorably backward—for, despite the achievement of the 1984 trade surplus, not a single cent had been knocked off Brazil's $100-billion international debt for five years.

It is a long time since anyone expected Brazil to become a world power by the year 2000, the goal of its military leaders in 1964. But, with its enormous resources and prodigious optimism, Brazil still promises enough to bring out the best in its people. The country's immediate future, however, hangs on the whims of its creditors, not the efforts of its citizens, and few see how it can shift its immense mountain of debt. Further pressure from the world's bankers could release social and political forces that would severely shake the entire edifice of a society still only on the edge of maturity. Were that to happen, Brazil could yet turn its back on the world and attempt to go it alone. And if Brazil were to suspend its international debts, there is little anyone could do about it. □

Beneath lofty trees spangled with yellow lights, the streets of Salvador are jammed with traffic, while pleasure seekers stroll the boulevards. Founded in 1549, the city was the capital of Brazil until 1763, when it lost its status to Rio de Janeiro.

BUILDING ITAIPU:
A COLOSSUS AMONG DAMS

Photographs by Vautier-de-Nanxe, Paris

When the first turbines came into operation in 1984, the Itaipu Dam on the Paraná River between Brazil and Paraguay became the largest hydroelectric installation in the world. As part of a long-term plan to harness Brazil's immense water resources, the dam, which cost an estimated $18 billion, was intended to supply one fifth of all Brazil's electricity needs and thus reduce reliance on imported oil.

Everything about Itaipu is gargantuan: Its potential daily generating capacity is enough to light a city the size of London. The dam's mighty walls—almost 550 feet thick—extend for 4.8 miles and rest on a maze of concrete-filled tunnels. The 3.1 million cubic feet of concrete needed to construct the dam—sufficient, it is said, to build eight medium-size towns—were supplied by three on-site cement plants and carried to the construction area in overhead gondolas traveling on seven aerial cables stretched high above the dam. A town, comprising 500 housing units, four hospitals, schools for nearly 16,000 pupils, as well as movie theaters and restaurants, was built for the 37,000 construction workers and their families.

Itaipu is only one of several huge civil-engineering projects undertaken in the last two decades in Brazil. Others include the Tucurui Dam in the northeast, the fourth largest in the world, and the 3,480-mile-long Trans-Amazonian Highway, which links Brazil's western frontier with the Atlantic seaboard.

Against a stormy sky, workers on the Itaipu Dam erect a web of steel reinforcing rods, which will be embedded in concrete. In recompense for arduous 11-hour shifts and a high risk of injury, the men earned twice what they would have on ordinary construction projects.

A 10-ton mobile crane, dwarfed by the unfinished concrete ramparts of Itaipu's main structure, is hoisted to a higher level. From its foundations on the Paraná river bed, the dam rises 735 feet, making it more than half as tall as New York's highest building, the World Trade Center.

A forest of reinforcing rods, scaffolding, cranes and ladders stretches between the riverbanks during the building of Itaipu's powerhouse, contained in the dam's main wall. The structure will house the generators and 18 turbines, each with a daily 700-megawatt capacity.

A workman uses a tool to remove air pockets from fresh concrete poured around the base of towering reinforcing rods.

Balanced on a framework of planks, dam workers smooth down the concrete floor of the Itaipu power station.

Illuminated by the white flare of his torch, a welder works through the night on a massive grid of reinforcing rods. In order to complete the dam on schedule, work continued round-the-clock throughout construction.

The brown water of the Paraná River, diverted during the dam building, churns through a temporary channel in the partially completed barrier.

In a vacant lot in Bahia, barefoot youngsters play a spirited game of soccer. Almost every Brazilian supports one of the country's 20,000 soccer teams, whose artistry and skill have produced many of the finest players in the world and made Brazil a leading soccer power.

A CULTURAL MELTING POT

Once a year, the world is given a tantalizing glimpse of a uniquely Brazilian event, the great Dionysian revel that is Carnival in Rio de Janeiro. It has been called "the greatest show on earth," and in scale and sumptuousness, it far outstrips other Christian pre-Lenten festivals such as Fasching in Munich or Mardi Gras in New Orleans and Nice. In Rio de Janeiro, the Carnival festivities start on the Saturday before Ash Wednesday, and for the next four days and four nights, the entire city abandons itself to a collective frenzy of music, dance and eroticism.

During the daytime, exotically costumed revelers parade through the streets, singing and dancing. Every evening in the theaters and nightclubs, bands play Carnival music while merrymakers in fancy dress dance through the night. And on Sunday evening, there begins a gigantic parade that lasts until Monday afternoon. Each of the 80,000 citizens of Rio who takes part belongs to one of 40-odd samba schools, neighborhood clubs that spend every weekend of the year planning and rehearsing their performances for those few hours. With big cash prizes at stake, the schools compete to create the most inspiring pageant of dancing and of elaborately decorated floats.

Nowadays, Rio's Carnival is geared to the media and substantially funded by the Ministry of Tourism. The professional input in the parade's set pieces grows yearly and spontaneity corre-spondingly diminishes. But Brazil's other cities have their own smaller and less publicized versions of Rio's Carnival, and these are still dedicated to impromptu merrymaking. The best of the lesser carnivals are thought to be those of Salvador, Brazil's first capital, and Olinda, the colonial city adjacent to the port of Recife; there, the atmosphere is authentic and good humor prevails.

Both Portuguese and African contributions are discernible in Carnival—but in fusing they release entirely new energies. The earliest Portuguese settlers were accustomed to letting off steam with pranks and horseplay—throwing flour or soot at their neighbors, for example—in the last few days before the onset of Lent. By the mid-19th century, however, the rough games were being replaced by religious pageants and masked balls. Meanwhile, African slaves entered into the spirit of the season, celebrating with drum music and dances—including one called the samba, which had Angolan antecedents and simulated the movements of copulation. But until well into the 20th century, this music was only one genre among many, which included guitar works and thoroughly European waltzes and polkas. Then, in 1917, a samba called *pelo telefone*—meaning "on the telephone"—was recorded for gramophone and became an instant hit. It was the first of many sambas to achieve renown in Brazil and beyond. Deriving from African drum rhythms and Portuguese folk songs, the syncopated music was joyful, brash and optimistic. The samba took Brazilian Carnival by storm and has remained its most characteristic feature ever since.

Carnival, and the samba that throbs at its heart, encapsulates Brazil's eclectic and vigorous culture. The varied heritages derived from the Brazilian population's European, African and American roots have been woven together so intricately, and transformed so radically by the shared climate, geography and social history, that something entirely new has emerged. Brazilian culture is sensuous, vital and defiantly different. Brazil's contributions to classical music, to literature and to the visual arts are by far the most significant of any South American country, and Brazilians are very well aware of the fact. But the nation's most characteristic achievements are at the popular level, the samba being the supreme example.

The confidence and great pride that Brazilians feel in their national culture is a fairly recent, 20th-century phenomenon. For most of the first four centuries after the Portuguese discovered Brazil, the inhabitants looked toward the continent of Europe for inspiration. With few exceptions, their buildings and paintings closely followed Portuguese styles, their reading matter was imported. Brazil's language was Portuguese, albeit a progressively softer and more musical version of the mother tongue, which eventually absorbed many African and Amerindian words. The Portuguese also gave Brazil its religion, and without a doubt, Roman Catholicism was their most pervasive cultural legacy to their colony.

In the early colonial days, the Cath-

olic Church's monopoly of ideas appeared to be virtually total. Fernando de Azevedo, in his seminal study of 1943, *Brazilian Culture,* writes: "So intimate and constant are the relations between the development of religion in Brazil and that of the intellectual life in our first three centuries, that one cannot for that long period separate one from the other."

But when the first African slave ships began arriving in Brazil, other currents began to flow beneath the surface of society. The slaves, too, took most powerful expression in religion. The African cults proved as enduring as the official faith. Today, one of the most characteristic aspects of Brazilian cul-

tural life is its blend of religions, which exist side by side in remarkable harmony. Brazil is the most populous Catholic country in the world, with 90 percent of its people professing, if not actually practicing, Roman Catholicism. But a growing number of people, perhaps as much as 20 percent of the population, are members of spiritist cults, and many more, while not actually belonging to a cult, participate in major spiritist festivals.

What was crucial for the development of Brazil's culture was that Portuguese Catholicism was never as rigid or as exigent as the Catholicism brought by the Spanish to South America. Its lack of formality, its plasticity,

left room for the absorption of other influences. This is not to say that the Church in the early days of Portuguese colonization did not attempt to impose its own cultural hegemony. Catholic missionaries, particularly the Jesuits, had indeed been ruthless about converting the Amerindians, assuming that the Indians had no art and no culture whatever, that their minds were a *tabula rasa*—or "blank slate," a tablet scraped bare of all concepts and beliefs. The African slaves brought in to work on the sugar plantations received the same overbearing treatment. Many were baptized en masse by priests as they were forced onto the slave ships in African ports; in any event, they were

all obliged to become Christians, and to observe Christian practices when they arrived in Brazil.

But the slaves brought with them their own, often sophisticated, cultures: Some were adherents of old African religions with formalized rituals and pantheons. They often came from ancient polities where there were strong traditions of music, dance and orally transmitted poetry and where highly skilled sculptors worked in wood and metal. Some of the slaves were Muslims, and a few were more literate than their masters.

They may have crossed themselves dutifully before images of the Virgin Mary during the day, but at night, they

played the drums that they kept hidden in the slave quarters. In secret, they worshipped their old gods—Xangô (god of thunder and lightning), Ogun (god of war) and Oxōssi (god of hunters). From these practices, which were officially suppressed by the Catholic Church, was later to emerge the sorcery of Brazil's spiritist cults.

Even in Brazil's early days, black culture found subtle ways of infiltrating the lives of the Portuguese ruling classes. The black cooks who ran the kitchens of the white houses would modify traditional Portuguese and Amerindian dishes to suit their own tastes, introducing the hot peppers, okra, ginger, melon seeds and *dendé* oil of their native Africa, so creating a characteristic Brazilian cuisine. White children were reared in intimate contact with black people, who served in various domestic capacities in their houses. Black women were their wet nurses and their nannies. Black children were their childhood playmates. Black women were their first sexual partners in youth, their mistresses in adulthood, often their confidantes, their source of solace or special magic in time of trouble. The chief black servant of a household often gained a status not far below that of her white mistress; and it was not unusual that, for as long as she lived, the black nanny who had brought up a white child was the most trusted person in the child's life.

The Catholicism practiced in the 17th-century sugar plantation homes was always ready to absorb these outside influences, probably not so much for liberal reasons, but more out of an amiable insouciance. The Brazilian sociologist Gilberto Freyre, in his book *The Masters and the Slaves,* describes the religion of the plantation owners as "domestic, lyric and festive Christianity, with its humanly friendly male and female saints and its Our Ladies as godmothers to the young."

It was a faith that had little interest in strict orthodoxy, but adapted itself to the daily needs and the morals of the plantation owners—and these, to say the least, were far from the European ideal. Priests were often the sons of plantation owners and officiated in the private chapels attached to their great houses. Very often, the padres performed a valuable educational function by giving lessons to the children of the house—including the slave children—but, like their secular peers, they frequently had mistresses and illegitimate

children—and seemed unaware of any moral inconsistency.

Moral rectitude was certainly not a feature of the gold rush that followed the age of the sugar plantations and brought new wealth to the interior of Brazil. But one side effect of the 18th-century gold boom was a spate of building—including some magnificent churches. In the burgeoning towns of Minas Gerais, many old churches were refurbished, and many new ones were built in the baroque and rococo styles popular in Europe and particularly appropriate to the exuberant prosperity of the successful prospectors. Ringed by hills, Ouro Prêto—once known as Vila Rica, or "Rich Town," and at that time capital of the region—still resembles Braganza or other baroque towns in northern Portugal. Its steep streets

At a stall selling paperbound copies of popular stories, a vendor entertains the crowd by giving a public reading through a microphone muffled with a handkerchief. The booklets are commonly called *cordel,* or "string," literature, from the way they used to be displayed in street markets.

are still paved with blocks of iron slate and granite, and there are 13 splendid churches, some with interiors almost entirely covered in gold leaf.

It was in Ouro Prêto that a genius of American colonial sculpture and architecture was born in 1738. He was the illegitimate child of a Portuguese carpenter and a black slave woman. His name was Antônio Francisco Lisbôa, but he is always called O Aleijadinho, or "The Little Cripple," because of the progressive mutilating disease, probably leprosy, that attacked him in middle age, withered his fingers and disfigured his face.

The boy learned his craft from his father and was soon much in demand as a sculptor of religious images and also as a church architect. As his health deteriorated, he became unable to walk and his face was such a loathsome sight that he chose to work behind screens. His terrible afflictions notwithstanding, he went on working tirelessly, turning out scores of sculptures with the help of his favorite slave, Mauricio, who is reputed to have had to tie chisel and mallet to the stumps of O Aleijadinho's useless hands.

The results are strikingly original. Unlike other 18th-century church sculptors, O Aleijadinho did not idealize his men and women. His distorted, angular figures are reminiscent of those painted by El Greco nearly two centuries earlier. The facial features of his statues are based on those of the people—often rather frightening in their aggressiveness—who surrounded him in the harsh environment of this gold-obsessed mining town.

He was already an old man when he created his masterpiece: a series of sculptures for the Sanctuary of Bom Jesus de Matozinhas at Congonhas, a

small town near Ouro Prêto. Arrayed on the terraced forecourt of the church are 12 larger-than-life soapstone statues of the Biblical prophets. And for the six chapels that line the approaches to Bom Jesus, O Aleijadinho created seven groups of carved figures representing scenes of Christ's Passion, all executed in life-size polychromed wood. These intense, tormented figures express the suffering in the sculptor's own life, as well as the suffering of the pilgrims who, for nearly two centuries, have come to pray at the shrine.

. Pilgrimage is still a powerful tradition in rural Brazil. It is an expression of the Catholicism practiced by the countryfolk who, probably because of a perpetual shortage of priests, have retained many of the practices and superstitions of the 17th century. One fa-

mous mecca for pilgrims is the city of Bom Jesus da Lapa on the São Francisco River in Bahia: Twice a year, tens of thousands of people assemble here, drawn to its miracle-working image of Christ and a network of underground caverns that have been turned into shrines. Some have come on foot from as far as 500 miles away, to fulfill a vow or pray for divine help.

Other shrines, such as Our Lord of Bonfim in Salvador, are famous for working miracles all year round. The Bonfim has a special "museum of miracles" for votive offerings from people who have experienced faith healing. The museum has a collection of wax replicas of heads, arms, legs, hearts, breasts—the parts of the body that were afflicted before a visit to the Bonfim brought about a miraculous cure. Here

one may purchase ribbons inscribed with the name of Our Lord of Bonfim, which are tied around the believer's left wrist. He or she can then make three wishes, all of which will be granted by the time the ribbon wears away and falls off the wrist—usually a matter of three months or so—and it is a strict condition that the ribbon fall off of its own accord. At any given moment, perhaps half the population of Salvador can be seen wearing frayed and faded ribbons. Most people maintain that their wishes have been answered, but they also say that it is important to keep the wishes within reasonable bounds, or they may not be fulfilled after all.

Strangely, the Bonfim is also known as the church of Oxalá, or "the Lord of Creation," in the pantheon of Candomblé, one of the Brazilian cults that grew

5

The foremost Brazilian composer of the 20th century, Heitor Villa-Lobos (1887-1959), works on one of his scores, cigar in mouth. A number of his world-famous compositions draw on the rhythms and melodies of Afro-Brazilian folk music and employ Amerindian instruments.

out of the African religions. Candomblé originated in northeastern Brazil, among the Yoruba peoples brought from the Guinea coast of Africa; another cult, Macumba, developed in the south out of the religions of the Bantu slaves imported from Angola. Both cults revolve around mediums able to contact the spirit world. Practitioners may heal sickness through the aid of their familiars or summon devils to perform black magic.

In modern-day Brazil, the Candomblé and Macumba cults are not confined to the descendants of African slaves or even to the poor; many highly educated, white, middle-class Brazilians slip away every month or so to attend one or another Afro-Brazilian magic rite. This development constitutes not so much an abandonment of Catholicism as a supplement to more orthodox religious beliefs, for many adherents of the Afro-Brazilian cults remain fervent Catholics. In the Bonfim church, each January sees an important festival for members of both the Christian and Candomblé congregations, in which Catholic priests and the Candomblé spiritual leaders, who are known as "mothers of saintliness," walk hand in hand.

African culture, which is powerfully expressed in the religions of Brazil today, also informs some of the nation's best literature. Indeed, Brazil's first great literary figure, Antônio de Castro Alves, was himself the son of a slave. He published a volume of poems in 1870, and others appeared after his death in 1871. They expressed his anger at the hardships suffered by his people in slave ships and on the sugar plantations. Castro Alves was the first really popular poet in Brazil, and his great abolitionist poem, *Voices from Africa,* is still recited in family gatherings and public meetings.

In the realm of fiction, the first important Brazilian works were written by Joaquim Maria Machado de Assis, the offspring of a black house painter and his Portuguese wife. Machado, orphaned and epileptic, fought his way out of the slums of Rio de Janeiro by working first as a typesetter, and then as a proofreader and journalist. As the 19th century drew to a close, he wrote a succession of novels whose skeptical

and ironic tone disguised a fine sensitivity toward the human condition. One of his masterpieces, *The Heritage of Quincas Borba*, tells of a man who dissipates his fortune on a married woman who fleeces and then deserts him. The hero of another, *Dom Casmurro*, schemes for years to escape from a seminary to be reunited with his childhood sweetheart, only to endure the tortures of an unhappy marriage.

It was left to another of the 19th-century realists, Aluísio Azevedo, to produce the most powerful Brazilian novel about the love of a black man for a white woman, *O Mulato*. Azevedo came from São Luís, capital of the state of Maranhão. His account of life in São Luís was so realistic, and was considered so scandalous at the time he wrote it, that he was obliged to leave his native city and move to Rio de Janeiro. After writing two more widely acclaimed novels, he entered the diplomatic service—and never published another book.

Castro Alves, Machado and Azevedo were figures of the Brazilian Empire. For all their individual talent, their work did not yet add up to a national school, and the other writers of their era tended to be strongly Eurocentric. It was only after Brazil became a republic in 1889 that the literary search for the country's soul began in earnest. An early indicator of the emerging artistic nationalism was the publication in 1902 of *Rebellion in the Backlands* by Euclides da Cunha. Cunha's epic account of a historical event portrayed the men who participated in it as characters shaped by their labors, as pioneers in a ruthless land.

The event behind *Rebellion in the Backlands* was an uprising in 1897 led by the religious fanatic Antônio Maciel, who was known to his followers as O Conselheiro, or "The Counselor." A native of Pernambuco, he had taken to a nomadic, ascetic life in the back country. In the barren wastes 375 miles from Bahia, a band of impoverished peasants gathered around him and recognized him as their chief. They helped him build a settlement that they hoped would become a Utopian community of peace and justice. When he later came into conflict with the governor of Bahia and was ordered to move, O Conselheiro and his few thousand followers defied the authorities and fought off

A soapstone statue of the prophet Hosea, carved by the 18th-century sculptor O Aleijadinho, stands before a church in Congonhas. The twisted angle of the statue's legs is believed to reflect the artist's deformity.

the army of police that had been sent to forcibly eject them.

In March 1897, some 1,500 soldiers, with four pieces of artillery, attempted to put down the rebellion, but were totally defeated. Eventually, the federal government was obliged to dispatch an expeditionary force of 5,000 men to crush the rebels. Their fortress was besieged and captured in September of 1897; disillusioned and despairing, O Conselheiro died shortly before the final assault.

This saga might easily have become just another footnote to Brazilian history had it not been for Cunha, a newspaper correspondent from São Paulo who accompanied the army during the campaign. The book that he wrote about the affair has been described as the greatest of Brazilian classics and the bible of Brazilian nationality. Although the book is a work of fact, it reads like fiction. The great Viennese critic, Stefan Zweig, who spent his last years in Brazil before his death in 1942, considered that the work gave "a complete psychological picture of the Brazilian soil, the people and the country."

Euclides da Cunha had profound sympathy and understanding for the rebellious inhabitants of the stricken northeast, who were struggling for survival in the face of a hostile environment and an uncomprehending government. He observed that these hardy frontiersmen would give every indication of overwhelming exhaustion until the very moment of having to make an effort. But: "In this weakened organism complete transformations are effected in a few seconds. All that is needed is some incident that demands the release of slumbering energies. The fellow is transfigured . . . and the awkward rustic unexpectedly assumes the dominating aspect of a powerful copper-hued Titan, an amazingly different being, capable of extraordinary feats of strength and agility." Understandably, Cunha was dismayed that such people had to die in the name of law and order, for they constituted "the very core of our nationality, the bedrock of our race."

Rebellion in the Backlands was undoubtedly a milestone, but Brazilian literature had to wait until the 1920s before it came of age. The Brazilian modernist movement arrived with a clash of cymbals in the form of manifestos and provocations such as Mário de Andrade's *Hallucinated City:* "I insult the bourgeois! O nickel-plated bourgeois, O bourgeois-bourgeois! The well-made digestion of São Paulo!" The movement culminated in a Week of Modern Art held in the city of São Paulo in 1922, to celebrate a century of Brazilian independence. Out of the many readings, exhibitions, conferences and statements of that week emerged an awareness that Brazil had something special to offer within the framework of Western culture. Writers resolved to keep up with the European avantgarde while tackling specifically Brazilian themes at the same time.

Intrigued by the primitive, as were their European and North American contemporaries, Brazilian intellectuals and literati took a sudden interest in the poorest and previously most disregarded of all their country's many havenots: the Indians who lived, virtually without possessions, in the great rain forests of Brazil.

In the 19th century, a few Brazilian writers had affected a passionate interest in the Indians but it was badly informed enthusiasm: They romanticized the lifestyle of the Indians, portraying them as noble savages. Now, for the first time, Brazilians were prepared to take a realistic look at their compatriots. They recognized that the myths and music of the Indian people, their art and handicrafts, were the residual treasures of a highly complex, refined culture that had been 10,000 years in the making.

Anthropologists scoured the Indian villages, trying to record their legends and creation myths before the taletellers became corrupted by mass communications such as the radio. From the Tucano Indians of the northwest Amazon, for example, the anthropologists learned that: "The first men were sent to earth by the Sun Father, creator of the universe. They traveled in a great snake canoe in the form of an anaconda . . . These first men dispersed along the rivers and settled in the forests to people the earth."

There proved to be much to learn from these secretive peoples. Sophisticated Brazilians discovered that the Tucano Indians of the upper Río Negro made some of the toughest, lightest and most elegant baskets in the world by skillfully braiding together a network of jungle vines; the Kadiweu of the Paraguay River painted abstract patterns on deer hide, which Picasso or Paul Klee would have admired; the Kuikuru of the Xingu River produced dance masks that might easily have been painted by Miró.

One outcome of the new respect for the Indians was the novel *Macunaíma: Hero Without a Character,* by Mário de Andrade, which was published in 1928. Exploiting the racy, idiomatic language of several different regions of Brazil, it recounts the fantastic travels of its eponymous hero, a cult figure of Indian Tupi mythology. Almost aggressive-

ly, the book takes the stance that Brazil has a language, a mythology and a way of life quite separate and distinct from those of Europe.

One of the most self-critical books about the Brazilian character was also written in 1928. Its author was an elderly businessman from São Paulo, Paulo Prado. His *Portrait of Brazil,* subtitled *Essay on Brazilian Melancholy,* states its thesis in a memorable opening sentence: "In a radiant land there lives a melancholy people." Prado develops the argument that the principal characteristics of the Brazilians are sexuality and envy. In Prado's opinion, sexual passion wore out both the Portuguese and the Indians, and from the hunger for gold there resulted the sadness of the new race, to which the African brought "his sickly collaboration as an exile and a slave."

The pessimism of Prado's book was an anomaly, and subsequent writers swung back to more joyful topics. The 1930s and 1940s saw a succession of vigorous novels and poems on Brazilian regional themes. Brazil's best-known postwar novelist is Jorge Amado, whose *Gabriela, Clove and Cinnamon* celebrates the zest for life of the beautiful mulatto of the title. Every image, every personality, is drawn from Amado's birthplace—Bahia. A Communist, Amado in his early novels stereotyped the virtuous and suffering peasants and the evil powermongers. But the novels of the 1950s and 1960s, including *Gabriela, Clove and Cinnamon* and *Dona Flor and Her Two Husbands,* take a more humorous view of the rural establishment's pretensions.

Like Brazil's writers, the country's artists and musicians discovered a national identity in the 1920s. They, too, drew

heavily on African traditions and self-consciously incorporated Indian motifs into their work.

It was from the Indian tribes of the Amazon and the Mato Grosso that Heitor Villa-Lobos, Brazil's foremost composer, learned the use of the exotic percussion instruments that snap, rattle and scrape in some of his instrumental compositions. In the same works, he employed African drum beats, patterns of sound that, though extraordinarily complex, never fail to set the feet moving. The alternation of African dance rhythms with the more brittle, delicate sounds of the Indian instruments is one of Villa-Lobos' characteristic hallmarks.

Although he was born in Rio de Janeiro and spent most of his life in that city, Villa-Lobos was drawn toward Amerindians and Afro-Brazilians by a musical tropism that no Brazilian composer can escape for very long. Even when he was not employing native tambours and rattles, or trying to capture "the sounds of the jungle at night," he would base his songs and orchestral scores on the folk music he had heard in the back country when he traveled through the northeast as a young man. Indeed, if any one individual can embody the *genius loci* of modern Brazil it is the prodigious Villa-Lobos; he is, without a doubt, is one of the most original and versatile composers in the history of music.

By no means all of his work is dominated by percussion rhythms; much of it is subtle and elusive, such as the famous *Bachianas Brasileiras No. 5,* the fifth of his "Brazilian Tributes to the Spirit of Bach," in which a solo soprano hums a Bachlike aria to the accompaniment of eight plucked cellos, which divide up the chords between them like

5

a giant guitar. It is a sound utterly unlike anything else to be heard in modern music. And then a contrasting *Dansa* evokes the sound of an Indian flute in the depths of the forest: "Ireré, my little nestling from the wilds of Cariri . . . Sing and enchant me . . . *La, lia! lia! lia! lia!*"

The career of Heitor Villa-Lobos illustrates both the delights and difficulties attendant on being a composer in a land rich in musical materials but poor in financial opportunities for serious musicians. Born in 1887 of a Spanish father and a Brazilian mother, he studied cello and piano along traditional European lines before discovering the mother lode of Brazilian folk music. Before long, he was writing the first experimental pieces in which Indian and Afro-Brazilian elements were joined to the Impressionist harmonies of Claude Debussy.

The trouble was that Rio had no audience for music of this sort during the early years of the 20th century. Villa-Lobos was obliged to eke out a living by playing the cello in the orchestra of a silent-movie theater. The only people who could be expected to understand his compositions were musical sophisticates from Europe who were accustomed to hearing similar experiments from composers such as Maurice Ravel and Igor Stravinsky.

One such European was the pianist

122

Artur Rubinstein, who went to Rio on a concert tour in 1919 and happened to hear about Villa-Lobos from mutual friends. They arranged for him to be introduced to the young Brazilian composer, whom he found to be "a short man of dark complexion, clean shaven, with dark disorderly hair and large sad eyes, but his hands were his most attractive feature with their lovely shape, sensitive and alive." When Rubinstein asked whether he had written anything for the piano, Villa-Lobos said moodily: "Pianists have no use for composers. All they want is success and money."

Understandably annoyed, Rubinstein went back to his hotel room. At eight o'clock in the morning a few days later, Rubinstein heard a knock at his hotel-room door. On opening the door, he related, "I saw to my surprise 10 or 12 men carrying different musical instruments. One of them was Villa-Lobos, who tried to convey to me in his mixed French and Portuguese that he was here to comply with my wish to hear his compositions. 'My friends are occupied during the day,' he said. 'This is the only time they are free to play.' "

Although it was very early in the morning, Rubinstein agreed to listen to several of Villa-Lobos' compositions. Some were easy to understand, others were difficult, but as Rubinstein recalled, "I was convinced that I was facing a great composer."

It was the beginning of the composer's rise to international prominence, for Rubinstein also prevailed on one of Rio's wealthy art patrons to provide financial support so that Villa-Lobos could study in Paris. He went on to show the whole of Europe a new kind of dissonant, folk-based music, and after he returned to Brazil and until his death in 1959, he was the best known and most often played of the South American composers.

The modernist movement of the 1920s that inspired Villa-Lobos also set off a flood of talented painters and sculptors. They stayed in the vanguard of international stylistic movements but chose Brazilian themes as their subject matter. The foremost among them was Cândido Portinari. Born in 1903 to a poor Italian immigrant family, Portinari, like many Brazilian writers of the period, was fascinated by the condition of the rural poor and underprivileged. An immensely versatile figure, he painted most often in a stylized form of realism that conferred majesty even on everyday subjects. His images—coffee plantations, peasants in the northeast—were unmistakably Brazilian. From the late 1930s onward, Portinari was practically Brazil's official artist, being commissioned to produce many large-scale murals for the public buildings that were beginning to spring up in profusion in Brazil.

Brazil's spectacular modern architecture is one of the most potent expressions of its 20th-century artistic confidence. In many respects, Brazil has been the architect's dream country, with ample space, relatively few building regulations and little opposition to new ideas from cautious traditionalists. A key figure in the nation's architectural development was Lúcio Costa, who, together with the Swiss architect Le Corbusier and other contributors, was responsible for the Ministry of Education and Culture in Rio de Janeiro. This building, completed in 1942, is considered a landmark in Brazil's architectural history.

It was Costa who, at the end of the 1950s, drew up the masterplan for Brazil's architectural showpiece, the new

On the rear wall of the Church of São Francisco near Belo Horizonte, a tiled mural by Cândido Portinari portrays the life of Saint Francis. Completed in 1945, the mural was at first thought as shockingly avant-garde as the church, the work of Brazil's eminent architect Oscar Niemeyer.

5

capital of Brasília. The buildings within his grand design, executed by architect Oscar Niemeyer, were acclaimed by critics and colleagues as highly original masterpieces of contemporary architecture. Excoriated by some observers as a concrete jungle lacking a human dimension, admired by others for its bold abstract forms, Niemeyer's achievement in Brasília has attracted worldwide attention.

The best Brazilian architects have refused to follow global fashions blindly. Back in the 1930s and 1940s, when the functionalist creed was being preached most insistently, a school of Brazilian architects rejected orthodoxy and instead espoused organic forms and attempted to integrate buildings into their natural surroundings.

Later, the native originality expressed itself in unexpected geometry. Among the most striking recent creations are Sérgio Bernades' low-slung, wheel-shaped Hotel Tambaú, which was built on the beach in João Pessoa, and Glanco Campelo's exhibition palace for the Administrative Center of the state of Bahia—a massive concrete shape suspended in midair between two conical towers.

In Manaus, a brilliantly innovative architect, Severiano Mario Porto, has been building homes and offices using the native materials of the Amazon in a new and exciting way. His roofs and porches rest on rough-hewn logs from the jungle; the walls and floors are of wood or tile, resulting in a relaxed and comfortable ambiance. Porto air conditions his houses in the natural way, employing the Amazon winds for cross ventilation, and he allows rain to fall through special openings in the roof to water his indoor gardens.

A number of other idiosyncratic Bra-

BAHIA'S CULINARY HERITAGE

The most famous regional cuisine of Brazil is that of Bahia in the northeast. Here, many distinctive dishes evolved in the colonial plantation kitchens. Because wheat flour and meat were often in short supply, the African slave cooks turned instead to the wealth of seafood caught in coastal waters and to local produce such as manioc flour, sweet potato, coconut, pineapple and palm oil. To flavor these dishes they used spices from their native Africa to produce dishes such as *abará*, shrimp and black beans, and *vatapá*, a stew of fish, shrimp, ginger and coconut milk.

A rich variety of produce is displayed in street markets in Salvador. A man sells watermelons *(near right);* a shopper considers a purchase at a spice stall. Near the beach, tables are piled with fruit and vegetables, while two fishermen *(far right)* tempt a motorist with their catch of spiny lobsters.

zilian architects are providing living spaces that are as welcoming as Porto's. Zamine Cladas, for example, makes use of unexpected combinations of exposed concrete and local wood for his country houses, while one of the houses created by Gerson Castelo Branco, on the beach at Piauí, was inspired by the design of the sailing boats common in the region. Each of these architects combines thoroughly modern techniques with the priceless heritage of local materials and traditions.

Brazilian high culture is constantly drawing upon the art of the ordinary people. For in this vast and diverse country, culture is the very stuff and substance of daily life, and by some strange law of compensation, Brazil's most disadvantaged inhabitants are also the possessors of some of its greatest cultural riches.

Brazil has a strong tradition of popular painting and sculpture, for example, which is barely influenced by international fashions or the burden of art-history tradition. One of the most talented of the untutored primitives was Djanira da Mota Silva, who was a descendant of Indians and Viennese immigrants. She exhibited her work for the first time in 1942 and very quickly achieved international fame. Mota Silva's strongly toned, flatly rendered two-dimensional figures and landscapes are filled with an innate lyricism. In the 1970s, another primitive artist,

Iracema Arditi, drew wide acclaim for her vividly colored paintings of flowers and tropical gardens.

But nowhere is the strength of Brazilian folk culture more obvious than in the field of popular music, which has become the country's best-known art form internationally and which draws its inspiration from a seemingly bottomless well of folk songs and dances. African influences predominate in the peculiarly Brazilian shapes and rhythms of the samba and the bossa nova, meaning "new skill."

The samba is simply a dance in two-part time, but it is what happens to the basics that counts: The secret of its fascination lies in the syncopations, the deviations from the norm. There is a saying among Brazilian musicians: *"Samba e coisa seria"*—"the samba is a serious matter." There are innumerable varieties of the urban as well as the rural samba—usually named for their character, instrumentation or place of origin: the *samba de viola* (for a kind of guitar), *samba de chaula* (a very sexy version), "samba from the upper town," and so forth.

At Carnival time, whether in Salvador, Rio or elsewhere, there is a samba for everything. Yet rarely will a samba be heard the same way twice, since the music as well as the dances and costumes are constantly being updated and refurbished, adding new fillips of excitement to the existing formulas.

Although the music of Carnival tends to be a rough and ready kind, it has always fascinated the cognoscenti among musicians. The classic musician's account of the Rio Carnival was written by the French composer Darius Milhaud, who visited Rio during the Carnival season of 1917 and "immediately sensed the mood of crazy gaiety that possessed the whole town." One of the favorite amusements of the dancers, he noted, was to improvise words to a repeated tune. "The singer has to keep on finding new words, and as soon as his imagination begins to flag, someone else takes his place."

In the beginning, Milhaud found the complexities of the tango rhythms of his day difficult to define. "There was an imperceptible pause in the synco-

An agile practitioner of *capoeira*—a form of ritual combat devised by African slaves—does a handspring to avoid an opponent during a bout in Salvador. Movements are accompanied by a man playing a tambourine and two boys plucking *berimbaus*—single-wire, bowlike instruments.

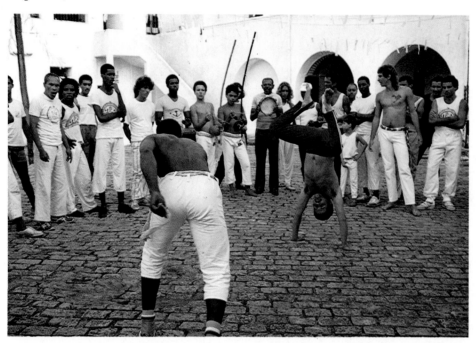

pation, a careless catch in the breath, a slight hiatus which I found difficult to grasp," Milhaud wrote. Eventually, however, he mastered the knack of playing the Carnival music on the piano—with their syncopated rhythms that ran from one hand to the other—by listening to a popular pianist whose "elusive, mournful, liquid way of playing also gave me deeper insight into the Brazilian soul."

The samba tradition that Milhaud observed continues to this day, changing and developing just as pop music evolved from the sound of Elvis to that of the Beatles and beyond. A major development occurred in the late 1950s with the bossa nova movement. While the classical samba has a strong melodic line, the bossa nova de-emphasizes the tune, so as to integrate it more closely with the other musical parameters—harmony and rhythm.

These days, the samba struggles to maintain its popularity in the face of rock music, and its devotees today are older than those of the 1930s and 1940s. But the sound of Brazilian rock has itself been influenced by the samba tradition: One of the musical heroes of modern Brazil, Gilberto Gil, sings rock songs grafted onto the rootstock of Carnival music: "From the city runs electricity in my brain; from the cars run gasoline in my veins . . . I am the electric man. Come and get a shock!"

Whatever the future direction of Brazilian popular music, it is certain to be ubiquitous. Music pulses through every corner of Brazil; it is as taken for granted as the sun. In every bar, someone will be playing the guitar; in every restaurant, a singer will be performing. On the beach, someone will pick out a rhythm on a drum and in no time, it will be echoed up and down the shore by

other sun worshippers. Even the traveler on a bus finds the whole vehicle rocking rhythmically as, one by one, the passengers take up a popular tune and sway to the beat.

Nothing can drown the Brazilians' love of music, but in the late 20th century they have developed two competing passions: television and soccer. Brazil now has one of the largest television networks in the world. Three quarters of Brazil's urban households and a fifth of its rural households have television sets. The most popular programs are the soap operas of extraordinarily high quality produced in Rio and São Paulo. A number of them have been sold abroad, and foreigners have found themselves becoming almost as addicted to these slices of Brazilian life as are the Brazilians themselves.

Soccer is Brazil's national obsession, and it is no accident that among the largest and most impressive buildings in the country are the immense soccer stadiums that can be found in every city worth its salt. Brazilians are famous for bringing soccer to new heights of skill, developing an unrivaled repertoire of kicks, dribbles and swerves. For Brazilians, soccer is more an art form than an aggressive sport and the crowd judges the play with the appreciation of connoisseurs.

Though tense with excitement, soccer matches are invariably good humored. Some of the spectators wave huge flags, others belt out samba rhythms on drums and trumpets. When the player with the ball evades an opponent with a spectacular piece of footwork, no ugly insults are heard from the supporters of the opposition. Instead, as if acknowledging a victorious toreador at a Spanish bullfight, the crowd cries with one voice *"Ole!"* □

Passengers aboard ship on the Madeira River, a tributary of the Amazon, lie in colorful hammocks slung above the deck. Light, portable and ideal for use in a hot climate, the hammock is an Amerindian artifact that has been readily adopted throughout Brazil.

The white robes of a Carmelite friar highlight the opulent gold and marble ornamentation of the baroque sacristy in Salvador's Convento do Carmo. Founded in 1586, the convent—now a museum—is a monument to the great wealth and power of the Roman Catholic Church in Brazil.

LAND OF MANY GODS

With more than 90 percent of its 130 million population professing the Roman Catholic faith, Brazil claims to be the world's most Catholic nation. Every town and village has its own patron saint whose festival is marked with processions and public celebrations, and each year millions of the devout go on pilgrimages to the country's holy places. Catholicism is the official state religion, and yet 30 million or more Brazilians exercise their legal right to freedom of belief. Moreover, they see no contradiction in being Catholics and, at the same time, members of one of the mystical sects that originated in Africa or in Brazil itself.

Such heterodoxy owes much to the historical tolerance of Brazilian Catholicism, which has embraced both African religion and Indian beliefs and absorbed their spirits and deities into its cosmology. The Church authorities encourage spiritists, such as followers of Macumba and Candomblé, to play an active part in Christian ceremonies and festivals.

Its baroque contours ablaze in the January night, Salvador's Church of Nosso Senhor do Bonfim is lighted for an annual festival combining Catholic and Candomblé elements. Candomblé followers identify Jesus Christ with Oxalá, their supreme god.

Three pilgrims sit impassively at Padre Cicero's birthplace in the village of Crato, some 15 miles from his church at Juàzeiro. A bust of the priest stands on the table behind them, protected by a plastic shroud and surrounded by vases of flowers.

A SHRINE TO PADRE CICERO

The village of Juàzeiro do Norte, in the hot, dry province of Ceará, is one of Brazil's foremost places of pilgrimage. Here, in 1889, a priest named Padre Cicero was administering communion to Maria de Araújo when she fell to the ground and the wafer dropped from her lips, covered in blood. Padre Cicero believed this was a miracle, that the communion wine had turned into Christ's blood, but the Church authorities refused to confirm it. When thousands of believers hastened to Juàzeiro and there were reports of new miracles, the padre was ordered by his superiors to leave the village. But, encouraged by his supporters, Padre Cicero decided instead to break with the Church and declared himself mayor of Juàzeiro. He ruled the area for two decades, and troops sent to evict him were repulsed. Yet Padre Cicero's faith proved so inspiring that, before he died in 1934, he was reconciled with the Church authorities.

In Juàzeiro's main square, thousands of visitors stream past an enormous statue of Padre Cicero. A typical street stall (below) offers plaster models of the famous priest clutching a bright red missal. His effigy stands cheek by jowl with images of the Virgin Mary and other sacred figures.

RITUAL OFFERINGS TO A SEA-GODDESS

The millions of Brazilians who are adherents of the gods and spirits of African cults are by no means confined to the descendants of slaves. Initiates come from every class and color, and many regard the synthesis of African religion and Christianity as Brazil's true national religion. Indeed, African gods have become identified with Christian saints: Yemanjá, goddess of the sea, is linked with the Virgin Mary, while Ogun, god of war, is associated with Saint George.

In Macumba, as in many other cults, initiates seek possession by the spirits in order to request their assistance or advice. Drumming, chanting and dancing all help to create a trancelike state in which such possession can take place, and the atmosphere of frenzy is heightened by the sacrificing of small animals.

A young woman *(below)* undergoes the first stage of initiation into the Macumba cult: being bathed in the purifying water of the sea. A lock of her hair will be cut off, and during the next three weeks, she will learn the elaborate chants and dances of the cult before becoming a full member.

On New Year's Eve, Macumba followers create an impromptu shrine on the beach at Rio de Janeiro and prepare a toy boat as an offering to Yemanjá. At midnight, they will launch the boat and carry flowers into the waves, hoping the goddess will grant their wishes during the coming year.

133

SUMMONS TO THE SPIRITS

A Hollywood-style temple at the Valley of the Dawn, a high desert plateau 25 miles from Brasília, is the home of a spiritist cult founded in the 1960s by a Brazilian mystic named Tia Neiva (Aunt Snow) and her lawyer husband, Mario Sassi. Claiming descent from beings who arrived from a distant planet some 32,000 years ago, they acknowledge the existence of Christ but teach that the world is entering a new era of widespread sickness and anxiety. By dispelling evil spirits from the earth, they hope to ease this change and bring comfort and self-fulfillment to the suffering. An endless stream of pilgrims, many of them poor and infirm peasants, visit the temple to witness ceremonies—which are performed by up to 3,000 initiates—and to purchase souvenirs, such as portraits of Tia Neiva and bottles of "curing" water.

A cult member shows young pilgrims a statue of White Arrow, the master of the solar system in his incarnation as a 16th-century Bolivian Indian chief who resisted the Spanish conquest. He was so named because his arrows were never red with blood: His victories were won by diplomacy.

In an hour-long ceremony, male initiates dressed in heavy dark robes prostrate themselves on individual "tombstones" around a star-shaped lake, to draw the evil spirits from the earth. The women, wearing ethereal, brightly colored dresses, can then transmit the spirits to a safer realm.

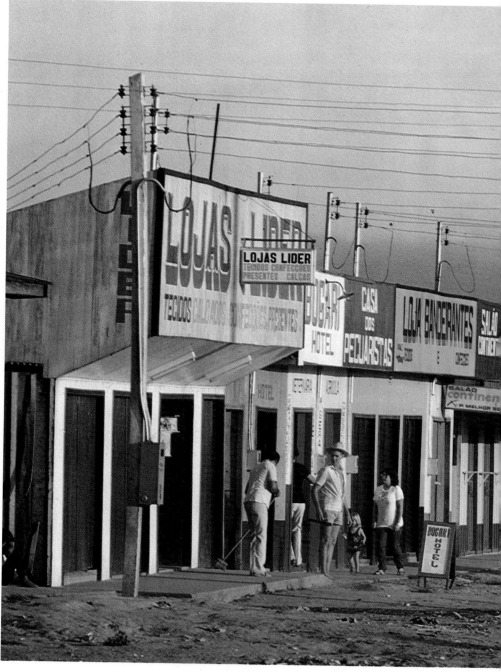

OPENING UP THE LAST FRONTIER

On Christmas Day 1541, a 60-man party of Spaniards, led by a one-eyed conquistador called Francisco de Orellana, set out by boat down the Napo River in Peru to find food for their comrades. They were part of an expedition that had come to South America in search of rare spices and the fabled city of El Dorado but that was now marooned and starving in the foothills of the Andes. Orellana's group—which included a friar, Gaspar de Carvajal, who kept a record of the voyage—soon found food, but the men had lost the strength or the will to row back up the Napo. So they went on, drifting more than 870 miles downstream until, on February 11, they debouched into another river so large, so powerful, that they believed themselves doomed. "It came on with such fury and with so great an onrush," wrote Carvajal, "that it was enough to fill one with the greatest fear to look at it, let alone to go through it . . . and it was so wide from bank to bank from here on that it seemed as though we were navigating launched out upon a vast sea."

Swept along by the mighty currents, the Spaniards followed the river eastward. Hunger was their main threat. Sometimes they found Indians who were willing to give them food, and sometimes they raided villages to seize provisions by force, but when all other supplies failed, they were reduced to eating their belts and the soles of their shoes boiled with herbs. At last, eight months after leaving their comrades, the Spaniards sailed out of the river's mouth into the Atlantic, having navigated the great waterway for more than 2,400 miles.

They made their way up the coast of Venezuela to safety, bringing tales of real and imagined riches, of large cities glistening in white, and of fierce warrior women who, said Carvajal, "were very white and tall and had their hair braided and wrapped round their heads. They were very muscular and wore skins to cover their shameful parts, and with bows and arrows in their hands, they made as much war as 10 men." This account was carried back to Spain and so inflamed the imaginations of the members of the royal court that they named the river the Río de las Amazonas, after the warrior women of Greek myth.

The story of the Amazon, which starts with myth, continues with dreams—dreams of finding lost civilizations deep in the interior, dreams of turning "a land without men" into a homeland for "men without land," dreams, above all, of discovering great treasures in the wilderness. Here, in 1983, a 23-year-old gold digger at an open-pit mine found an 80 percent pure nugget weighing 137.3 pounds—part of a $500-million haul unearthed in the first three years of the mine's operation. Here, between 1970 and 1985, more than one million poor and dispossessed Brazilians settled to carve

An unpaved main street and frame buildings testify to the makeshift beginnings of a pioneer town in the state of Mato Grosso. In the vast northwest, new towns quickly spring up when settlers move in to seek a new life as ranch hands, small-scale farmers or prospectors.

6

a new life out of the wilderness. Here, the dreams of European colonists have made a nightmare for the Amazonian Indians, the main casualties in a centuries-long conflict between modern society and nature.

With an area in excess of 1.5 million square miles—nearly half the total area of Brazil—Amazonia is vast enough to accommodate the most grandiose of visions. If it were a country, it would rank seventh largest in the world, behind Australia but ahead of India. If all its trees were felled, one third of the world's forest area would have been lost, for Amazonia, as one 19th-century English botanist observed, is "clad with trees and little else but trees . . . enormous trees, crowned with magnificent foliage, decked with fantastic parasites, and hung over with lianas, which [vary] in thickness from slender threads to huge python-like masses."

In shape, Amazonia resembles an ovate leaf, with veins made up of more than 1,000 rivers converging on a central rib formed by the Amazon itself. Almost 4,000 miles long, the Amazon River is a little shorter than the Nile, but by any other reckoning, it is the greatest river in the world. It is estimated that the Amazon and its 1,100 tributaries carry down to the sea one fifth of all the fresh water in the world, discharging it at the rate of about 2.6 billion gallons per second from its mouth. So great is the flow that it pushes back the salty sea water for 100 miles offshore—a fact first reported by the man credited with finding the Amazon, the Spanish sea captain Vincente Yáñez Pinzón, who believed that he had discovered a fresh-water sea until he followed the silt-stained current into the main artery of the river.

Many of the Amazon's tributaries are mighty in their own right: There are 17 that are more than 930 miles long, and 10 that carry more water than the Mississippi. Oceangoing freighters can penetrate 2,200 miles up the main river to Iquitos, Peru, their passage assisted by the extremely shallow gradient of the watercourse, which drops less than 330 feet between Iquitos and the sea. In fact, were it not that the Amazon runs close to the equator, the flatness of its basin would ensure that most of Amazonia was permanently flooded and uninhabitable. As it is, the northern and southern tributaries rise in different hemispheres, with different rainy seasons, so only about half the rivers are in flood at the same time; thus the Amazon's annual rise and fall varies by only about 33 feet.

Another startling feature of Amazonia's rivers is their different colors. The Amazon itself, and most of the tributaries flowing from the Andes, are muddy brown in color because they are heavily laden with silt; this indicates that the Andes are young mountains from which soil nutrients have not yet been washed. By contrast, the Río Negro, which drains from highlands to the north, has black, clear water—indicating that the rocks at its source are so old that they have been leached of their minerals. The contrast is spectacularly evident where the Río Negro meets the Amazon near the town of Manaus: The two streams flow side by side for almost 50 miles with a clearly visible boundary between them.

This color-coding provides a simple clue to the geological history of Amazonia. The highlands from which the mineral-deficient waters flow were formed more than 200 million years ago, when the Amazon basin was still part of the supercontinent of Gondwanaland, which included Antarctica, South America, Africa, India and Australia. About 140 million years ago, Gondwanaland broke up, and the pieces drifted apart to become the present continents—huge rafts of relatively light granite rocks floating on plates of denser basalts.

South America split away from what is now Africa and drifted westward until it collided with the Nazca Plate, which forms the floor of the southeast Pacific Ocean. The impact crumpled the young rocks at the edge of the South American Plate into giant folds, creating the Andes. The mountains blocked the old mouth of the Amazon, damming the waters in a huge fresh-water lake, but some time in the last 50 million years—probably as a result of the continent's tilting to the east—the lake burst through the gap between the ancient rocks to north and south, creating the Amazon basin of today.

Three million years ago, further continental movement linked up North and South America at the Isthmus of Panama, providing a land bridge across which plants and animals could migrate in both directions. About the same time, the earth entered the present geologic era of ice ages and interglacials, but Amazonia's position astride the equator meant that it escaped the killing cold, and much of the flora and fauna that evolved during the region's millions of years of isolation has survived into modern times.

Amazonia, in fact, is the most mature woodland on earth—more than 9,000 times as old as the forests of North America and Eurasia, which have established themselves only since the last Ice Age. It is the richest storehouse of genes in the world, with a bewildering

In the rain forest, a red bromeliad clings to a tree trunk 30 feet above ground. Like many other plant species in Amazonia's complex ecology, bromeliads draw all the nourishment they need from the rain-saturated air around them, using their roots only to attach themselves to their hosts.

abundance of animal, insect and plant species, many of them not yet classified. Approximately one tenth of all known species are found in Amazonia, including an estimated 80,000 plants, 1,500 fishes, 200 snakes, and almost one quarter of the world's total of 8,600 bird species. Seven hundred species of butterfly have been collected within an hour's walk of Belém. More than 700 different species of fish—nearly as many as in all North American fresh waters—have been recorded within a 20-mile radius of Manaus.

And yet this luxuriant hothouse rests on very poor foundations; it is a trompe l'oeil of abundance painted by nature to disguise its basic infertility. Only the 4 percent of Amazonia that is flooded by the silt-rich rivers of the Andes has truly fecund soils; the rest, leached by eons of tropical rains, is about as fertile as a brick. Some scientists describe the region as a "desert covered with trees." The Amazon rain forest is an amazing balancing act in which all the species play mutually dependent parts. It is luxuriant because every resource of nature passes through the ecosystem; nothing is wasted. Every scrap of nutrient, every sunbeam, every drop of water is processed in elaborations of chemistry and behavior that make Amazonia the world's greatest biological laboratory.

In this miracle of mutual adaptation, only the highest trees—ranging from 115 to 150 feet—get the full benefit of the equatorial sunshine. Their fruits and leaves support colonies of monkeys, snakes and birds, which seldom leave the forest canopy. Lower down is a second layer of trees, more tolerant of shade, which grow to heights of between 20 and 65 feet and house their own animal denizens. Scrambled

The leisurely curves of the mighty Amazon river wind eastward toward the Atlantic Ocean, more than 200 miles away. Fed by 17 major tributaries, the

4,000-mile-long Amazon drains an area larger than Europe; huge tracts of the basin are still only partially explored and settled.

through and over these layers are numerous symbiotic climbing plants, ferns, orchids, algae and mosses, feeding on one another and at the same time interdependent. The forest floor is gloomy, for only about 10 percent of the sun's light is able to reach this far; and it is strangely uncluttered, because almost everything consumable, even a falling leaf, is recycled into the biomass before it reaches the ground. As a result, the soil is thin and the roots of the trees often penetrate no deeper than two feet into the ground. Even the biggest trees rely to a large extent for their support on the lianas that stretch from trunk to trunk.

Into this fragile and complex world came human beings, between 20,000 and 40,000 years ago, adapting their way of life to fit the contours of nature. Amazonia's Indians, descendants of the Mongolian Asians who crossed into the Americas by way of the Bering Strait during the Ice Age, have traditionally practiced a hunter-gatherer economy that makes no serious inroads on the forest's resources.

Traditionally, the 180 or so Amazonian tribes, who speak nearly as many languages and dialects, live in groups seldom larger than 200, in large communal houses with sections for each family to sling its hammocks—an Amerindian invention. Nearby they clear a small patch by slashing and burning the trees and undergrowth. Here they grow manioc, a tuber whose bitter poisons have to be squeezed out before it is edible; but most of their food comes from the forest itself. Fish are usually the protein staple, and the Indians have many ways of catching them—by netting, trapping, shooting with bows and arrows, paralyzing with poisons derived from any of a hundred toxic plants, and luring with lights or special whistles and calls.

Land animals of all sizes are also hunted and eaten—from piglike capybaras, which are actually rodents, to tiny tree frogs the size of a thumbnail. If game is scarce, the forest provides fruits, nuts and edible grubs for gatherers skilled enough to find them and experienced enough to distinguish the poisonous from the nonpoisonous.

Nearly all work is done communally, but tasks are divided between the sexes. The men hunt, defend the tribal territories and build the houses, while the women tend the crops, care for the babies and cook. Political structures are rudimentary, and there are no real social divisions within a tribe: Even headmen have only limited influence. The only person in a community with a specialized role is the shaman—a healer and an intermediary between the tribe and its spirit gods, with whom he speaks in a trance that often is induced by hallucinatory drugs.

Every 10 years or so, the group abandons its settlement and moves to another part of the rain forest. The decision to leave is usually made collectively by the men, who will consider whether their manioc plots are losing their fertility, whether their houses are beyond repair, and whether game is becoming scarce. When they go, the forest soon reclaims their land.

Consciously and unconsciously, the Indians keep their populations at a level that is in balance with the availability of resources. Some women take a drink distilled, appropriately, from the passion flower, which appears to stop ovulation the way modern oral contraceptives do. Some tribes, such as the Tapirapé, who live near the Araguaia River in the southeastern part of Amazonia, practice selective infanticide. The women of the Tapirapé tribe are not allowed to have more than three children or more than two of the same sex, and unwanted babies are left to die in the forest. Numbers are also kept stable by intertribal battles that result from territorial rivalry. Among the Yanomami Indians in the north, for example, about one quarter of the males meet with violent deaths.

The actual number of Indians living in Amazonia is difficult to estimate because some areas of rain forest are still unexplored and may harbor hitherto unknown tribes—such as the 95-strong group of Arara Indians who were discovered in 1984 in the state of Pará. But even if more tribes are found, it is unlikely that the total population exceeds 200,000—a pathetically small remnant of the estimated two to five million Amerindians who inhabited Brazil at the time that Orellana made his epic navigation of the Amazon.

The first objective account of Amazonia's Indians was provided by a Jesuit priest, Father Cristóbal de Acuña, who accompanied a Portuguese expedition that traveled the length of the Amazon between 1637 and 1641. Acuña described how one Indian tribe kept ponds stocked with thousands of turtles near their villages and how another produced pottery delicate enough to rival Chinese ceramics. But on the return journey, he witnessed the savagery with which the Indians were treated by Portuguese slave traders from Belém, a settlement established in 1616 on the Amazon estuary. Father Cristóbal watched in horror as one gang rounded up Indian men while allowing their own Indian auxiliaries to rape the women; and as the expedition neared

AMAZONIA'S GOLDEN MOUNTAIN

A prospector at the Serra Pelada mine glances up warily as he sluices a box of dirt for grains of gold. Some of the makeshift methods used for recovering gold have changed little in centuries. Here, a cooking pot peppered with holes in its bottom is used to disperse the water from a hose.

In January 1980, a tree on the Serra Pelada, a low mountain more than 300 miles south of the mouth of the Amazon, blew over in a storm. An amazed rancher, according to one story, found several gold nuggets as big as his fist in the tree's roots, and so set off a gold rush that within a month had attracted 10,000 prospectors. Impoverished peasants, illiterates from city slums, as well as lawyers and teachers, flooded in to stake claims and tear into the mountainside for the precious metal. The rowdy, gun-toting colony that sprang up had all the flavor of a *(continued)*

An army of diggers toil inside the mud-filled pit that was once the Serra Pelada mountain. In spite of its anarchic appearance, the mine is divided into more than 1,000 claims.

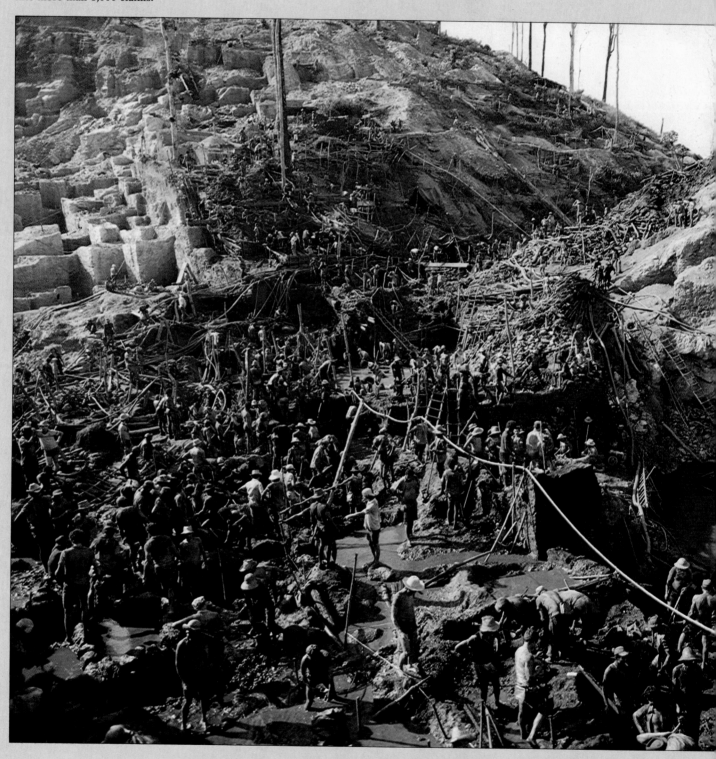

Caked with red earth, two prospectors *(right)* emerge from the mine carrying sacks of dirt. The rough ladders provide their only means of access to and from the mine 200 feet below.

California gold-rush camp of the 1850s, with gambling, prostitution and bitter feuds over claims.

Five months later the army moved in to bring order. Women and alcohol were banned from the site, and claims were set at 65 square feet per person. Gangs of 20 to 30 miners were hired by each claim owner, usually for a share of the profits, to dig and pan for gold dust. A few miners have become very wealthy overnight—an estimated one billion dollars' worth of gold, or more, was extracted in the first four years—but, for the majority of diggers, striking it rich remains a tantalizing dream.

A prospector waits while his gold dust is weighed by a government official. Before he is given a receipt for its worth and the money is deposited in his account, the gold will be checked with magnets in case it has been adulterated with metal filings.

6

Belém, he found that the whole area around the settlement had been denuded of its native population.

The Jesuit missionary Father António Vieira, who arrived in 1653, preached fiery sermons against the slave traders. "All of you are in mortal sin; all of you live in a state of condemnation; and all of you are going directly to hell," he thundered. Yet in their desire to "save" the souls of the Indians, the Jesuits directly contributed to their decline by encouraging them to leave the forest for mission villages, where they died by the thousand from European diseases against which they had no resistance. Nor did the Jesuits' denunciation stop the exploitation of Amerindian labor.

The real wealth of Amazonia was discovered by European naturalists, who began arriving in the region in the mid-18th century. To them, the rivers and their companion rain forests were a cornucopia of scientific marvels. One of the first and most important was the brilliant French polymath Charles Marie de la Condamine, mathematician, cartographer, astronomer and naturalist. He arrived in Brazil in 1743 and mapped the Amazon with remarkable accuracy. While studying its flora and fauna, he also investigated some of the poisons used by the Indians on their arrows and blowgun darts, and how they fished by beating the surface of the stream with certain creepers that left a chemical in the water to stun the fish. From the cinchona tree, he collected seeds that the Indians used as a prophylactic for malaria; the drug later came to be known as quinine. From the tree that the Indians called "the wood that weeps" he collected a milky sap that amazed him by its elasticity. He took samples back to Paris, but it was more than 100 years before the invention of the automobile created a huge demand for latex.

La Condamine was followed in 1800 by the German naturalist and explorer Friedrich von Humboldt, who investigated native poisons and tested the voltage generated by electric eels, after he had stepped on one of these brutes and received a shock that affected him for a day "with a violent pain in the knees and in almost every joint."

The most complete and valuable studies of Amazonia's natural history were made by two self-taught English scientists: Henry Walter Bates, a former hosier's apprentice, and Alfred Russel Wallace, who started his career as a surveyor's assistant. They met by chance in Leicester, and finding that they shared a fascination for the Amazon, they sailed for Belém in 1848, hoping to support themselves by sending plant and animal specimens back to the British Museum and the Royal Botanic Gardens at Kew at a few pennies apiece. For reasons that were not disclosed, they both chose to go their own ways soon after they reached South America, although they remained lifelong friends.

Bates spent 11 years in Amazonia, amassing a collection of 14,712 species, of which 8,000 were new to science—including bird-eating spiders as big as a fist. "One day," he recorded in his vivid and delightful *The Naturalist on the River Amazons*, "I saw the children belonging to an Indian family who collected for me with one of these monsters secured by a cord round its waist, by which they were leading it about the house as they would a dog."

Wallace's expedition lasted for four years, and his studies of the distribution and divergence of rain-forest species planted the seeds of a theory about evolution by natural selection that closely paralleled Charles Darwin's epoch-making work. In 1858, both men delivered papers to the Linnean Society in London, and although Darwin was credited with the discovery of the laws of evolution, Wallace never displayed any resentment, telling his old friend Bates: "I could never have approached the completeness of his work."

But many explorers sensationalized their accounts of Amazonia, describing it as a "green hell," a "wilderness of fools" or a "lost world" swarming with man-eating snakes, bloodthirsty head-hunters and lustful Indian women. One of the more scholarly of these travelers was former President of the United States Theodore Roosevelt, who made an expedition in Mato Grosso, where a river he discovered still bears his name. Amazonia, he averred, was the "world's last true frontier."

Just before World War I, when Roosevelt was adventuring in Amazonia, most of the vast region was, indeed, unknown to any besides the Amerindians who lived there, and it was almost completely untouched by the industrial world. Even the rubber boom, which had lasted a scant 30 years and had swollen the population of Amazonia by 90,000, had not seriously encroached on the forest. No roads had been built, for the raw material was transported by steamers down the river; no plantations had been cleared, for the industry depended on tapping the sap of trees that grew wild in the forest. Even the extravagant city of Manaus, built by the barons of the rubber industry, had reverted to an isolated outpost.

An attempt to revive the industry was made in 1924 when the state of Pará

146

gave Henry Ford 2.5 million acres to establish a rubber plantation. He planned to regain Brazil's former position as the world's leading rubber producer, but his trees, planted in neat lines and tended by workers lodged in a specially built town called Fordlandia, lacked the protection they had in their natural state and were highly vulnerable to disease and pests. In 1946, Ford pulled out and sold the project to the Brazilian government for $250,000. The company's investment had been more than $30 million.

So, once again, the vision of an El Dorado had disappeared into the green vastness. The rain forest was left to a few immigrant rubber tappers stranded after the collapse of the rubber industry, and to a trickle of landless peasants from the backlands of the northeast hoping to find some sort of living in Amazonia. To these people,

the Indians were a mortal foe, and they were treated accordingly. Small as the new settlers' numbers were, the Indians, armed only with bows and arrows, were beginning to be driven from their traditional hunting grounds.

The first major initiative to protect Brazil's indigenous population was undertaken at the turn of the century by a young army officer called Cândido Mariano da Silva Rondon. He was given the job of mapping parts of the wilderness and establishing telegraphic links between settlements, but in the course of his travels, he met several Indian tribes and grew to appreciate their cultures. In 1910, he persuaded the government to set up the SPI, the Service for the Protection of Indians.

Appalled by the brutality with which the encroaching settlers treated the native population, Rondon set himself the task of creating a society in which

whites and Indians would coexist peacefully, with Indians being given their own land until they could be assimilated into the rest of Brazilian society. First he had to establish friendly contact with the forest dwellers, and he did this by sending assistants to leave gifts such as axes, cooking pots and mirrors near Indian settlements. It was dangerous work, demanding considerable self-sacrifice, for Rondon strictly enforced his slogan: "Die if necessary, but do not kill."

His efforts were recognized worldwide; in Brazil he was promoted to the rank of marshal, and the Amazonian federal territory of Rondônia was named after him. But after his death in 1958 the SPI became corrupt. A decade later, it was disbanded after a commission of inquiry found that it had collaborated with land speculators in the massacre of entire tribes by bombing

6

and machine-gunning, using poisoned candy to kill infants and deliberately spreading disease through gifts of infected clothing.

Claudio Villas Boas, one of three brothers who continued Rondon's work through a new agency, FUNAI, the National Indian Foundation, delivered a sad epitaph on his mentor's work: "He ended his long and noble life in 1958, covered in glory, without realizing that all his work on behalf of the Indians had been turned against them. He had given them land: It was the signature of their death sentence. . . . Once the Indians were tamed by a man of noble spirit, they were then defenseless in the face of the adventurers who arrived hotfoot after him."

Large-scale encroachment on the Amazon rain forest by land speculators, cattle ranchers and land-hungry peasants started in the early 1960s, after the construction of the Belém-Brasília road, "the spine of Brazil." The human influx was given fresh impetus in 1966 by the new military administration when it launched *Operation Amazonia,* an ambitious plan to promote settlement in the region and integrate it fully into the economy. SUDAM, the Superintendency for the Development of the Amazon, was the state agency for this plan, which was built around generous tax incentives for investors. The scheme was very attractive to those who could afford to buy large tracts of land for ranching or land speculation. But it also attracted some foreigners, including the American entrepreneur Daniel K. Ludwig, whose ill-fated Jari project was intended to capture a major slice of the world market in wood pulp.

Underpinning *Operation Amazonia* was a massive program of road build-ing, which was pushed through at breakneck speed. In 1970, there were not even 1,000 miles of rough roads and fewer than 170 miles of paved roads in the whole of Amazonia. By the end of 1976, the network had been expanded to nearly 10,000 miles of dirt roads and more than 1,500 miles of paved highway—one third of this total made up by the Trans-Amazonian Highway, which stretches 3,480 miles from João Pessoa on the Atlantic coast to the Peruvian frontier in the west.

The new roads particularly helped cattle ranchers by making large-scale transportation of livestock to market economically viable. From 1966 to 1978, SUDAM gave the go-ahead to 358 ranches, for which it authorized tax rebates of $750 million. But many beneficiaries of this largess had no intention of using their land for cattle ranching: They regarded their spreads as little more than a speculative property investment obtained at a giveaway price. Of the 358 projects approved by SUDAM, it is estimated that only about 100 actually got off the ground, and few of these were successful.

Most of the ranchers knew little about tropical farming and made the mistake of assuming the rain-forest soil was fertile. Some cleared the land by the traditional slash-and-burn method; some used 100-yard-long chains slung between gigantic tractors to topple all the trees in their path; others sprayed defoliants from aircraft. In the first 10 years, more than 45,000 square miles of forest were cleared, and most of this land was intensively stocked with cattle. But with the protective canopy removed, the soil became impoverished within two or three years, and the ranchers' dream withered among weed growth and soil erosion. Some ranches

148

A gigantic wood-pulp mill sprawls incongruously in the primeval forest on the banks of the Jari River. Floated complete all the way from Japan in 1978, the plant was only part of a massive project to exploit Amazonia's resources; the plan also included mining and cattle ranching.

6

lasted only two years; others held out for as long as seven. One rancher, who bought almost 100,000 acres in north Pará, summed up the problems of farming in Amazonia: "It's like a marriage," he admitted ruefully. "It all goes well the first year or two, but then the problems begin."

By 1976, the failure of the cattle ranchers could no longer be ignored by the government, and in 1979, tax rebates for new ranches in the rain forest were discontinued. Attention now turned to the state of Rondônia on the southern fringe of the Amazonian rain forest, which was considered suitable for the resettlement of Brazil's 10 million landless peasants. A few individuals had started arriving in the area during the 1970s with the construction of the new roads; but after 1976, when the government promised the distribution of one million free land titles in Rondônia, the trickle became a torrent. In 1977, in one border post, 275 immigrants passed through a government processing center; in 1983, the number was 430,265.

The colonists were given 20- to 40-acre plots, laid out in a grid pattern that showed scant regard for the quality of soil or availability of water on individual holdings. Many of the plots proved to be unfarmable, and a large proportion of the colonists, exhausted by fruitless toil and tempted by cash offers for their land, sold out. Even so, the flood of migrants continued. Many spent up to four years on waiting lists for their allotments of land, eking out a living by working as day laborers for ranchers or established farmers.

To service the influx of settlers, new towns sprang up almost overnight; Rolim de Moura, for example, which was founded in 1978, had a population of 60,000 by 1985. Such towns look and behave very like the frontier towns of the American Old West as portrayed by Hollywood. Farm laborers, horseless equivalents of the cowboys, often work 12-hour days for three-month contract periods, without women or drink, and when they reach town they vent their frustration in wild and frequently violent orgies in the bars and brothels.

Another similarity with the Wild West is the conflict between the cattle ranchers and squatters. Some of the ranch owners buy their land without having seen it, and when they make their first visit they find it already occupied by peasants who, under Brazilian law, cannot be evicted without compensation if they have lived there for a year and a day. If the peasants have been living and farming in one place for more than 10 years without any contact with a landowner, the property becomes theirs.

But on this frontier, the law is not always observed, and dark tales are told of the prorancher bias of land apportionment officials and the corruption of the police and courts. Some ranchers, having failed to persuade peasants to leave their land, hire gunmen to eject them by force. Many peasant families have been illegally evicted from plots three or four times but cannot afford to contest their cases in court. In 1975, however, the Catholic Church established a national pastoral land commission, the Commissão Pastoral de Terra (CPT), to advise and assist the rural poor in standing up for their rights in land disputes. Headed by a number of radical priests, the CPT encouraged families to hold out on their plots, even if threatened by gunmen. In the 1980s, imbued with a new sense of defiance, peasants banded together against the ranchers' hired thugs; several fierce and fatal gunfights resulted.

Gold prospectors are another violent element in Amazonia. Attracted to the region for centuries, they have come in vastly increased numbers since gold was discovered at Serra Pelada in 1980. Within a week of when the first nugget was unearthed, 1,000 miners were on the site; within a month there were 10,000, and by 1984, there were 40,000 at work in a pit big enough to swallow one of the great pyramids. All work is done by hand, but since few claim owners can afford a large payroll, wages are paid in terms of percentage of the value of a strike—1 percent for a spoil carrier, perhaps, and 2 per cent for a digger; the terms are sometimes written on the wrapper from a cigarette pack or in the margin of a magazine.

On the Madeira River, on Brazil's Bolivian border, another 4,000 men are trying to get a share of the $300 million of alluvial gold brought up from the river bed each year. The gold is recovered using rafts and what are, in effect, huge vacuum cleaners worked by divers. It is dangerous work: The divers work six-hour shifts, often competing with rival teams poaching on their territory. Down there in the darkness, it is easy for air lines to become entangled, and just as easy for them to be cut by a resentful colleague. Officially, 20 divers died in 1984; the actual toll was much higher.

Of the estimated 250,000 prospectors chasing dreams in Amazonia, many operate in small teams in remote areas that are occupied only by forest Indians. These men go heavily armed against surprise attack and tend to regard any Indian they might encounter as an enemy to be shot on sight.

Less destructive of human life, but

Mourners in the state of Rondônia wait among ranks of recent graves while a richly decorated coffin is sealed before being lowered into the ground. Untimely death is common in Brazil's frontier regions, where disputes are often settled by gunfights.

150

potentially more damaging to the environment, are the large Brazilian and multinational mining companies that the government has been encouraging into Amazonia to exploit its massive mineral wealth; bauxite, iron ore, tin, manganese and diamonds are just a few of its underground resources. Bauxite mining and aluminum smelting started on a large scale in the early 1980s, and they were soon followed by the even larger Carajás mining project in the state of Pará, to the west of the Araguaia River, which contains the largest known reserves of high-grade iron ore in the world.

To exploit the iron ore of Carajás, which also contains huge deposits of other minerals, Brazil has built the three-billion-dollar Tucurui Dam, which will eventually flood 850 square miles of forest—and engulf the homeland of the Parakana Indians, one group of whom were discovered only in 1976. Until the 1970s, the whole tribe had numbered 700 to 1,000, living in three groups; but in 10 years, contact with alien diseases had reduced their numbers drastically, to about 300.

Since 1968, when the discredited SPI was replaced as the Indian protection agency by FUNAI, the Brazilian government has set aside large areas of Amazonia to shield the native population from settlers and developers. In 1980, FUNAI supervised four main parks—the Xingu and Aripuaña in Mato Grosso, the Araguaia in Goiás and the Tumucumaque in Pará—and 17 reservations, the combined area of which exceeded 36,000 square miles. In spite of this practical demonstration of concern for the Indians, however, FUNAI is often criticized for its contradictory roles—to preserve the life and culture of the Indians on the one hand, to integrate them into modern society on the other.

Some Indians who live in the parks and reservations have already been compromised by European civilization. The once warlike Kayapo tribe, for example, living in the Gorotire Reservation on the banks of the Xingu River, have given up bows and clubs, and their new symbols of manhood are hunting rifles and transistor radios. Young men now wear shorts instead of penis sheaths and have abandoned their tra-

With a cub on her back, this lumbering giant anteater is easy prey for hunters.

A giant otter surfaces in a pool of dark water.

A three-toed sloth, an almost-toothless herbivore, reaches out to grasp a meal of leaves.

Two capybaras wallow in water. Expert swimmers, they often are three feet long.

A giant armadillo, which may weigh more than 130 pounds, forages for food.

A jaguar lazes in a tree, but it is equally at home in water and often catches fish.

RARE BREEDS IN A THREATENED WORLD

For billions of years the Amazon rain forest has provided a stable environment in which plant and animal life have evolved in thousands of unique forms. But the forest ecosystem is so finely balanced that many species are interdependent; the loss of one can lead to the loss of another.

Human society barely disturbed this balance until the 1960s, when an accelerated program of building dams and roads and clearing the forest for ranches and mining made such serious inroads on the habitat of many animals as to threaten them with extinction. The arboreal sloth, for example, cannot easily cross new roads and so is cut off from some of its grazing grounds. This, in turn, deprives plants and insects that depend for survival on the nutrients in the recycled foliage provided by the sloth.

Other species are threatened by hunters after their meat: Capybaras, amphibious vegetarians that are the world's largest rodents, are widely eaten, and the giant armadillo is considered a delicacy by Indians. Jaguars and the giant otter are hunted for their fur and for sport, and the latter, once seen in many Brazilian rivers, is now found only in inaccessible parts of Amazonia. Many creatures—monkeys, exotic birds and even the giant anteater—have been reduced to pitifully small numbers by the desire for unusual pets.

There are now laws to protect endangered animals, but they are almost unenforceable in the 1.5 million square miles of the rain forest. Scientists fear that some animal and plant species will never regain healthy population levels, and will die out—with incalculable loss to humanity.

6

ditional lip disks because "you can't speak Portuguese when you are wearing one." The reservation now has churches, schools, mission houses and mobile health teams.

In any case, the parks and reservations may not be able to hold out against economic interests. When uranium was found on the Yanomamo Reservation in Roraima, the governor made his position clear: "I am of the opinion that an area as rich as this—with gold, diamonds and uranium—cannot afford the luxury of conserving a half-dozen Indian tribes who are holding back the development of Brazil."

Against pressures like these, the Indians are beginning to fight back, using white society's own political weapons. Their lead came from CIMI, the Catholic Church's body for Indian affairs, which was radicalized in the early 1970s by the charismatic bishop of São Félix, Dom Pedro Casaldáliga, who helped Indians set up regional, then national, assemblies where they could air concerns and grievances.

Frustrated, however, by what they regard as the government's reluctance to heed their demands, some Indians have used their newfound political sophistication in conjunction with direct-action tactics. For example, in April 1984, a group of Txukarramrae Indians near the Xingu River became exasperated with the government's delay in establishing a promised buffer zone to protect their territory from encroaching cattle ranches. In a dramatic move, they kidnaped three government officials and threatened to kill them if the zone was not demarcated immediately. The government, fearful of the political repercussions if the hostages were murdered, readily agreed to the demands.

This incident made international headlines, but by then media attention was focusing on a more general concern—the destruction of the rain forest itself and the possible consequences for the global environment. The forest not only protects the soil against erosion but also manufactures its own rain: Research has shown that moisture from leaves—either evaporated from them or released by transpiration—accounts for more than half the rainfall in Amazonia. This leads scientists to fear that a desert the size of Europe would be created if the region were to lose a lot of its tree cover.

There are fears, in addition, that deforestation could lead to a disastrous global warming by increasing the amount of atmospheric carbon dioxide, a heat trap that constitutes only 0.03 percent of the volume of the atmosphere but that absorbs 15 percent of the energy radiated by the earth. According to the most pessimistic forecasters, so much carbon dioxide would be released by burn-off and bacterial activity in the disturbed soil that temperatures would climb high enough to melt the polar ice caps, thus raising sea level by about 200 feet and flooding many of the world's major cities.

How much of Amazonia has already been destroyed is open to dispute. Apologists claim that only 3 percent has been cleared, while others say the figure is much greater and that the sensitive balance of the ecosystem has already been damaged beyond repair. These critics question why the forest needs to be disturbed at all. They point out that there is enough cultivable land outside Amazonia to give each Brazilian 2.5 acres—more land than is available in the United States. They point out that, despite the money poured into

A clearing breaches the forest canopy (*above*), where Amazonian Indians have erected a thatched *maloca*—a communal house for several families; in a nearby river, four girls kneel in a cloud of butterflies (*right*). Despite such idyllic scenes, contact with outsiders threatens their way of life.

the settlement of Amazonia, estimated at $12,000 per settler, the region still has only 4 percent of Brazil's population and produces only 2 percent of the country's gross national product.

It would be unrealistic to imagine that Amazonia could simply be handed back to nature, but the conservationists believe that it could be exploited in a much more thoughtful way, rather than being ravaged for purely short-term economic and political gain. The billions that were spent on a project such as Jari, for example, would have been better spent on developing sustainable methods of culling native hardwoods, for which world demand is high. The Amazon's huge stocks of fish could be a far more valuable source of protein than the expensively intro-duced cattle, which, fed on poor scrub, are fit only for hamburger meat.

Ecologists are concerned that Amazonia is being destroyed before anyone can find out what other valuable resources it has to offer; it would take scientists decades to evaluate the potential uses of its 80,000 plant species. According to Richard Schultes, a Harvard botanist who spent 13 years in Amazonia, the Indians—who use more than 1,000 native plants for medicinal and other purposes—may be the short-cut to unlocking the forest's secrets.

Already, Indian lore has given the world *curare,* from the *Chondodendron* and *Strychnos* plant species, which Indians use to paralyze game and which Western doctors use as a muscle relaxant for heart-disease victims; and *rote-none,* from the bark of two plants, used by Indians to paralyze fish and by the industrial world as a safe, biodegradable insecticide. Schultes also believes that plants used by the Indians as hallucinogens may be valuable tools in psychiatric research, and he has found a species of Amazonian palm that yields a high-quality edible oil almost indistinguishable from olive oil. Of the 3,000 plants identified as having anti-cancer properties, 70 percent are rain-forest species, a fact suggesting that Amazonia may yield a cure for one of the world's greatest killers.

Amazonia, in short, still has many treasures to give up—treasures that are potentially of far greater value to humankind than the El Dorado of the early explorers' dreams. □

ACKNOWLEDGMENTS

The index for this book was prepared by Vicki Robinson. For their help in the preparation of this volume, the editors wish to thank: José Luiz Barcellos Dias, Rio de Janeiro; Antonio Barros, Salvador, Brazil; Brazilian Embassy Information Department, London; Mike Brown, London; Martha de la Cal, Lisbon; Kate Cann, Guildford, Surrey, England; Canning House Library, London; Eduardo Castanho, São Paulo, Brazil; Windsor Chorlton, London; Nina Coelho, Salvador, Brazil; Vivaldo Costa Lima, Salvador, Brazil; John Cottrell, Weybridge, Surrey, England; Jane Curry, London; De Simoni Associados, São Paulo, Brazil; João Romeu Dutra, Porto Alegre, Brazil; John Gaisford, London; Helen Grubin, London; Caroline Hill, London; Institute of Latin American Studies, London; Michael Kepp, Rio de Janeiro; João Lacerda, Bagé, Brazil; Maria de Lourdes Noronha Pinto, Porto Alegre, Brazil; Fred Monteiro, Salvador, Brazil; Salvador Monteiro, Rio de Janeiro; Tony and Marion Morrison, Woodbridge, Suffolk, England; Museu de Arte Sacra, Salvador, Brazil; Museu Costa Pinto, Salvador, Brazil; Robin Olson, London; Sally Rowland, Saffron Walden, Essex, England; Antonio C. dos Santos-Vovô, Salvador, Brazil; Lito Sarmento Filho, Bagé, Brazil; Roberto Stern, Rio de Janeiro; Roberto M. Suñe, Bagé, Brazil; Deborah Thompson, London; Lynn Underwood, London; Varig Brazilian Airlines, London; Edgar Wallau, Porto Alegre, Brazil; Marlene Webber, Library of the Brazilian Embassy, London.

PICTURE CREDITS

Credits from left to right are separated by semicolons, from top to bottom by dashes.

Cover: J. Alex Langley from Aspect Picture Library, London. Front endpaper: Map by Roger Stewart, London. Back endpaper: Digitized map by Ralph Scott/Chapman Bounford, London.

1, 2: © Flag Research Center, Winchester, Massachusetts. 6, 7: Gerd Ludwig from Visum, Hamburg. 8, 9: Digitized chart by Ralph Scott/Chapman Bounford, London; Claus C. Meyer from Colorific!, London. 10-13: Loren McIntyre, Arlington, Virginia. 14, 15: Martin Rogers from Woodfin Camp Inc., Washington, D.C.; Digitized map by Ralph Scott/Chapman Bounford, London. 16, 17: Claus C. Meyer from Colorific!, London. 18: Cavan McCarthy from The Hutchison Library, London. 19: Digitized map by Ralph Scott/Chapman Bounford, London. 20, 21: Tony Morrison, Woodbridge, Suffolk, England. 22, 23: Claus C. Meyer from Colorific!, London. 25-29: Vautier-de-Nanxe, Paris. 30, 31: Claus C. Meyer from Colorific!, London. 32: Loren McIntyre, Arlington, Virginia. 34, 35: Claus C. Meyer from Colorific!, London. 36, 37: Rodolpho Machado from Colorific!, London. 38, 39: Claus C. Meyer from Colorific!, London. 40-41: The Financial Times/Robert Harding Picture Library, London. 42: Courtesy of the Bibliothèque Nationale, Paris. 44: Courtesy of the Collection of the Arquivo Historico Ultramarino, Lisbon. 47: Lithograph by Isidore Laurent Deroy from a watercolor by Johann Rugendas, Museu Raymundo Ottoni de Castro Maia, Rio de Janeiro, courtesy of Fundação Nacional Pró-Memória. 48: *Soldados Indios de Mogi das Cruzes*, lithograph from a watercolor by Jean-Baptiste Debret, Museu Raymundo Ottoni de Castro Maia, Rio de Janeiro, courtesy of Fundação Nacional Pró-Memória. 50, 51: Courtesy of the Museu Paulista, Universidade de São Paulo. 52: Courtesy of the British Museum (Natural History), London. 54: Medallion from the cloisters of the Jeronimos Church, Lisbon; *Vista de Aqueduto de Santa Teresa*, oil painting by Joaquim Leandro, courtesy of the Museu Nacional de Belas Artes, Rio de Janeiro—*Funcionario do Governo Saindo a Passeio* by Jean-Baptiste Debret, Museu Raymundo Ottoni de Castro Maia, Rio de Janeiro, courtesy of Fundação Nacional Pró-Memória. 55: *Week of Modern Art*, exhibition catalogue cover by Di Cavalcanti, 1922, courtesy of the Biblioteca Nacional, Rio de Janeiro—BBC Hulton Picture Library, London—The Photo Source, London. 57: The Burton Holmes Collection, Los Angeles, California, U.S.A. 58: Photo Maia from Foto Flash, Fortaleza, courtesy of the Museu Historico e Antoropologica do Ceará, Fortaleza, Ceará, Brazil; Film still from *Memória do Cangaço*, dir. Paulo Gil Soares, Cinemateca do M.A.M., Rio de Janeiro. 60, 61: John Moss from Colorific!, London. 62, 63: Homer Sykes, London. 64: Claus C. Meyer from Colorific!, London. 66: Sarah Errington from The Hutchison Library, London. 67: Vautier-de-Nanxe, Paris. 68: Nicholas Devore from Bruce Coleman Ltd., Uxbridge, Middlesex, England; Nobu Arakawa from The Image Bank, London; Sarah Errington from The Hutchison Library, London. 69: Fred Grunfeld, Majorca; Jesco Von Puttkamer from The Hutchison Library, London; Tony Morrison, Woodbridge, Suffolk, England. 70: Loren McIntyre, Arlington, Virginia. 71: Michael Boys from Susan Griggs Picture Agency, London. 72: Claus C. Meyer from Black Star/Colorific!, London. 73: Antonio Gusmão from Colorific!, London. 74, 75: Dr. Nigel Smith from The Hutchison Library, London. 77: Vautier-de-Nanxe, Paris. 78-85: Claus C. Meyer from Colorific!, London. 86, 87: Loren McIntyre, Arlington, Virginia. 89: Antonio Gusmão from Colorific!, London. 91: Claus C. Meyer from Colorific!, London. 92: Loren McIntyre, Arlington, Virginia. 94: Tony Morrison, Woodbridge, Suffolk, England. 95: Gerd Ludwig from Visum, Hamburg—Homer Sykes, London. 97: Vautier-de-Nanxe, Paris. 98, 99: Richard House from The Hutchison Library, London. 101: Vautier-de-Nanxe, Paris. 103: Claus C. Meyer from Colorific!, London. 104-111: Vautier-de-Nanxe, Paris. 112, 113: Claus C. Meyer from Colorific!, London. 114: Vautier-de-Nanxe, Paris. 115: Tony Morrison, Woodbridge, Suffolk, England. 116: Luiz Claudio Marigo from Bruce Coleman Ltd., Uxbridge, Middlesex, England. 117: Vautier-de-Nanxe, Paris. 118: Fred Grunfeld, Majorca. 119: The Kobal Collection, London. 120: Tony Morrison, Woodbridge, Suffolk, England. 122: *Café*, an oil painting, by Cândido Portinari, 1935, courtesy of the Museu Nacional de Belas Artes, Rio de Janeiro. 123: John Lewis Stage from The Image Bank, London. 124-126: Claus C. Meyer from Colorific!, London. 127: Michael Lange from Visum, Hamburg. 128, 129: Claus C. Meyer from Colorific!, London; J. Alex Langley from Aspect Picture Library, London. 130, 131: Vautier-de-Nanxe, Paris. 132, 133: Walter Firmo from Colorific!, London; Sebastian Barbosa from The Image Bank, London. 134, 135: Vautier-de-Nanxe, Paris. 136, 137: Michael Lange from Visum, Hamburg. 139-141: Loren McIntyre, Arlington, Virginia. 143-145: Vautier-de-Nanxe, Paris. 147: Loren McIntyre, Arlington, Virginia. 148, 149: Martin Rogers from Woodfin Camp Inc., Washington, D.C. 151: Claus C. Meyer from Colorific!, London. 152, 153: Alan Root from Survival Anglia Ltd., London; Keith and Liz Laidler from Survival Anglia Ltd., London (2)—Konrad Wother from Bruce Coleman Ltd., Uxbridge, Middlesex, England; Alan Root from Bruce Coleman Ltd., Uxbridge, Middlesex, England—Loren McIntyre, Arlington, Virginia. 154: T. Aramac from Colorific!, London. 155: Loren McIntyre, Arlington, Virginia.

BIBLIOGRAPHY

BOOKS
Amado, Jorge, *Gabriela, Clove and Cinnamon.* Trans. by J. L. Taylor and W. L. Grossman. London: Chatto & Windus, 1963.
Amado, Jorge, Oscar Niemeyer, et al., *Brazil.* London: Thames and Hudson, 1971.
Andrade, Geraldo Edson de, *As Festas Brasileiras de los Pintores Populares.* Rio de Janeiro: Imprinta, 1980.
Annuario Estatistico do Brasil. Brasília: Secretaria de Planejamento, 1983.
Annuario Estatistico do Brasil. Brasília: Ministerio do Industria e Commerçio, Conselho de Não Ferrosos e de Siderurgia, 1985.
Ayala, Walmir, *O Brasil por Seus Artistas.* Rio de Janeiro: Editora Nordica Ltda., no date.
Azevedo, Fernando de, *Brazilian Culture.* Trans. by William Rex Crawford. New York: Macmillan, 1950.
Barbican Art Gallery, *Portraits of a Country.* Catalogue of Pictures from the Gilberto Chateaubriand Collection, 1984.
Bastide, Roger, *Les Religions Africaines au Brésil.* Paris: Presses Universitaires de France, 1960.
Bello, José Maria, *A History of Modern Brazil, 1886-1950.* Trans. by J. L. Taylor. Stanford, California: Stanford University Press, 1966.
Bethell, Leslie, *The Abolition of the Brazilian Slave Trade.* Cambridge, England: Cambridge University Press, 1970.
Bethell, Leslie, ed., *The Cambridge History of Latin America.* Vol. 11. Cambridge, England: Cambridge University Press, 1984.
Botting, Douglas, *Rio de Janeiro* (The Great Cities series). Amsterdam: Time-Life Books, 1977.
Bourne, Richard, *Assault on the Amazon.* London: Gollancz, 1978.
Bourne, Richard, *Getúlio Vargas of Brazil.* London: Knight & Company, 1974.
Boxer, C. R., *The Golden Age of Brazil.* Berkeley, California: The University of California, 1962.
Braddon, Russell, Christina Dowell, Germaine Greer,

et al., *River Journeys.* London: BBC, 1984.

Bradford Burns, E., *History of Brazil.* New York: Columbia University Press, 1980.

Brazil. Geneva: Nagel's Encyclopedia Guide, 1980.

Brazil: A Geography. London: Brazilian Embassy, 1984.

Brazil: 1984. Petroleo Brasileiro S.A. Petrobras, 1984.

Brazil: State and Struggle. London: Latin American Bureau, 1982.

Brazilian Art. São Paulo: Ministry of External Relations, 1976.

Brooks, John, ed., *The South American Handbook 1983.* Bath, England: Trade & Travel Publications, 1983.

Calva, Ralph della, *Miracle at Joaseiro.* New York: Columbia University Press, 1970.

Carmichael, Elizabeth, and Stephen Hugh-Jones, *The Hidden People of the Amazon.* London: British Museum, 1985.

Carneiro, Edison, et al., *O Negro Brasileiro.* Rio de Janeiro: Cadernos Brasileiros, 1968.

Chandler, Billy Jaynes, *The Bandit King: Lampião of Brazil.* College Station, Texas: Texas A&M University Press, 1978.

Conrad, John Edgar, *Children of God's Fire.* Princeton, New Jersey: Princeton University Press, 1983.

Contas Nacionais, Annuario Estatistico do Brasil. Rio de Janeiro: Fundação Getúlio Vargas, 1984.

Cruz, Davidoff, *Divida Externa, e Politica Economica.* São Paulo: Brasiliense, 1984.

Cunha, Euclides da, *Rebellion in the Backlands (Os Sertões).* Trans. by Samuel Putnam. Chicago: Chicago University Press, 1944.

Degler, Carl, *Neither Black nor White.* New York: Macmillan, 1971.

Dickenson, J. P., *Brazil.* London: Longman, 1982.

Dorst, Jean, *South America: A Natural History.* London: Hamish Hamilton, 1967.

Dulles, John W. F., *Unrest in Brazil.* Austin, Texas: University of Texas Press, 1970.

Dzidzienyo, Anani, and Lourdes Casal, *The Position of Blacks in Brazilian and Cuban Society.* London: Minority Rights Group, 1979.

Fernandes, Florestan, *The Negro in Brazilian Society.* New York: Columbia University Press, 1969.

Flynn, Peter, *Brazil: A Political Analysis.* London: Ernest Benn, 1978.

Fodor's Brazil. New York: McKay, 1985.

Frater, Alexander, ed., *Great Rivers of the World.* London: Hodder & Stoughton, 1984.

Freyre, Gilberto:
The Mansions and the Shanties (Sobrados e Mucambos). Trans. by Harriet de Onís. New York: Alfred A. Knopf, 1963.
The Masters and the Slaves (Casa-Grande e Senzala). Trans. by Samuel Putnam. New York: Alfred A. Knopf, 1956.

Furtado, Celso, *Formação Economico do Brasil.* Brasília: Editora Nacional, 1984.

Goodland, R.J.A., and H. S. Irwin, *Amazon Jungle: Green Hell or Red Desert?* Amsterdam: Elsevier, 1975.

Görgen, Hermann M., *Brazil.* Innsbruck, Austria: Pinguin-Verlag, 1981.

Guppy, Nicholas, *Tropical Deforestation: A Global View.* Washington, D.C.: Foreign Affairs, 1982.

Harding, Bertita, *The Amazon Throne.* London: George G. Harrap, 1942.

Hasenbalg, Carlos A., *Race Relations in Brazil.* Albuquerque, New Mexico: Latin American Institute, University of New Mexico, 1985.

Hemming, John, *Red Gold.* London: Macmillan, 1978.

Henfrey, Colin, *The Gentle People.* London: Hutchinson, 1964.

Instituto Brasileiro de Análises Sociais e Economicas, *Dados da Realidade Brasileira.* Petrópolis: Vozes, 1982.

Instituto Brasileiro de Análises Sociais e Economicas, *Saúde e Trabalho no Brasil.* Petrópolis: Vozes, 1983.

Kent, Rockwell (introduction), *Portinari: His Life and Art.* Chicago: University of Chicago Press, 1940.

Lang, James, *Portuguese Brazil: The King's Plantation.* New York: Academic Press, 1979.

Lemos, Carlos, José Roberto, Teixera Leite, and Pedro Manuel Gismonti, eds., *The Art of Brazil.* New York: Harper & Row, 1983.

Lopes, Luiz Martins, *Bulletin Mensal da Faculdade de Economia e Administração de Universidad de São Paulo.* São Paulo: University of São Paulo, 1984.

Marshall, Andrew, *Brazil.* London: Thames and Hudson, 1966.

Merrick, Thomas W., *Brazil's Population since 1945.* Washington, D.C.: Unpublished paper from Population Reference Bureau, 1984.

Milhaud, Darius, *Notes sans Musique.* Paris: René Julliard, 1949.

Perlman, Janice E., *The Myth of Marginality.* Berkeley, California: The University of California, 1976.

Perry, Ritchie, *Brazil: The Land and Its People.* London: Macdonald Educational, 1982.

Phelps, Gilbert, *The Last Horizon: A Brazilian Journey.* Knight & Company, London, 1971.

Poppino, Rollie, *Brazil: The Land and the People.* New York: Oxford University Press, 1968.

Prado, Caio, Jr., *The Colonial Background of Modern Brazil.* Trans. by Suzette Machado. Berkeley, California: University of California Press, 1967.

Rabinovitz, Francine, and Felicity M. Trueblood, eds., *Latin American Urban Research.* Vol. 1. Beverly Hills, California: Sage, 1971.

Rivière, Paul, ed., *Amazonia, Orinoco and the Pampas.* Vol. 6 of *Peoples of the Earth.* London: The Danbury Press, 1973.

Rodrigues, José Honorio, *Brazil and Africa.* Berkeley, California: University of California Press, 1965.

São Paulo Justice and Peace Commission, *São Paulo— Growth and Poverty.* London: Bowerdean, 1978.

Schreider, Helen, and Frank Schreider, *Exploring the Amazon.* Washington, D.C.: National Geographic Society, 1970.

Schulthess, Emil, *The Amazon.* New York: Simon & Schuster, 1962.

Singer, Paul:
Crisis of Miracle. Rio de Janeiro: Paz e Terra, 1982.
Dominação e Disigualdade, Estructura de Classes, e Repartição de Renda no Brasil. Rio de Janeiro: Paz e Terra, 1981.

Skidmore, Thomas E., *Black into White.* New York: Oxford University Press, 1974.

Smith, Anthony, *Mato Grosso: Last Virgin Land.* London: Michael Joseph, 1971.

Sorjo, Bernardo, and Tavares de Almeida, *Sociedade e Politica no Brasil pos-64.* Ed. by Maria Herminia, São Paulo: Brasiliense, 1983.

Sterling, Tom, *The Amazon* (The World's Wild Places series). Amsterdam: Time-Life International, 1972.

Tradição e Ruptura. São Paulo: Fundação Bienal de São Paulo, 1984.

Wagley, Charles, *An Introduction to Brazil.* New York: Columbia University Press, 1971.

Wagley, Charles, ed., *Race and Class in Rural Brazil.* Paris: UNESCO, 1952.

Weil, Thomas E., *Area Handbook of Brazil.* Washington, D.C.: The American University, 1975.

Wellington, Sandra I., *The Art of the Brazilian Indian.* London: British Museum, 1978.

Worth, John D., *Politics of Brazilian Development, 1930-1954.* Stanford, California: Stanford University Press, 1970.

Zweig, Stefan, *Brazil: Land of the Future.* Trans. by Andrew St. James. London: Cassell & Company, 1942.

PERIODICALS

Art and Artists, Special Issue Brazil, April 1976.

Bury, John, "The Little Cripple: The Genius of Brazil." *World Review,* March 1951.

Conta, Manfred von, "São Paulo: Mammon und Macumba." *Geo,* May 1979.

Financial Times Special Reports:
"The Sleeping Giant Begins to Stir," December 7, 1982.
"Poised for a New Era," November 5, 1984.

Gaede, Peter-Matthias, "Os Abandonados: Die Strassenkinder von São Paulo." *Geo,* June 1985.

Georges, Eliane, "Brésil de Tous les Saints." *Geo,* May 1985.

"Itaipu: A Dam to Humble All." *Geo,* November 1981.

Kroll, Benno, "Manaus: Die Erben des Untergangs." *Geo,* October 1978.

Laxalt, Robert, "Last of a Breed: The Gauchos." *National Geographic,* October 1980.

Lea, Vanessa, "Brazil's Kayapo: Beset by a Golden Curse." *National Geographic,* May 1984.

Morrison, Tony, "Capital Achievement." *Telegraph Sunday Magazine,* June 16, 1985.

Rob, Gerda, "Salvador de Bahia: Stadt im Dunklen Schleier." *Geo,* May 1984.

Sa, Hernane Tavares de, "Metropolis Made to Order." *National Geographic,* May 1960.

Starbird, Ethel A., "The Bonanza Bean: Coffee." *National Geographic,* March 1981.

Villas Boas, Orlando, and Claudio Villas Boas, "Saving Brazil's Stone Age Tribes." *National Geographic,* September 1968.

INDEX

Page numbers in italics refer to illustrations of the subject mentioned.

A

Abaeté, Lagoa do, *39*
Abará, 124
Acuña, Father Cristóbal de, 142
Afro-Brazilian blacks: importation as slaves, 45, *47*, 48, 52, *54;* influence on cuisine, 115-116, 124; influence on literature, 118; influence on music, 113-114, 121, 125; intermarriage with whites, 24, 45-46, *69,* 74; percentage of population, 74; present-day social status, 63, 65, 73-74, 76-77; spiritist cults, 114-115, 117-118, *129, 132-133*
Afro-Brazilian Democratic Committee, 77
Agassiz, Louis, 53
Agricultural industry: in Ceará, *12-13;* exports, 22, 97-98; failure to develop, 97-98; and land distribution, 98; in Paraná, *21;* and work force, *8,* 22. *See also* Cattle; Rubber; Sugar
Aircraft manufacturing industry, 101-102
Alcohol fuel: distillation from sugar, 24, *97,* 100
Aleijadinho, O (Antônio Francisco Lisbôa), 54, 116-117; soapstone statue of Hosea by, *120*
Aluminum production, 100
Amado, Jorge, 24, 33; *Dona Flor and Her Two Husbands* (novel), 121; *Gabriela, Clove and Cinnamon* (novel), 121
Amazonia, 20-21, *30-31,* 138; climate of, 146; ecological concerns for, 154-155; economic boost for, *32-33;* failure of cattle ranches in, 148, 150, 155; flora and fauna in, *52-53,* 138-*139,* 142, 146, *152-153, 155;* gold mining in, 100, 137, *143-145,* 150; and Jari project, *87,* 148-*149;* land speculators in, 148; mining companies in, 151; population of, 30, 32; roads in, *map* 15; schools in, *75;* size of, 30, 138; timber reserves in, 21-22. *See also* Indians; Rubber industry; Trans-Amazonian Highway
Amazon River, 21, *140-141;* discovery of 138; first navigation of, 137; length of, 138; naming of 137; as tourist attraction, *10;* tributaries, 138
Américo, Pedro, painting by, *50-51*
Andrade, Mário de: *Hallucinated City* (novel), 120; *Macunaíma: Hero without a Character,* (novel), 121
Anteater, giant, *152-153*
Antonil (Italian Jesuit): quoted, 46
Araguaia Indian reservation, 151
Arara Indians, 142
Araújo, Maria de, 131
Architecture, 17, 19, 60, *123-*124
Arditi, Iracema, 125
Aripuaña Indian reservation, 151
Armadillo, giant, *153*
Arms industry, 101, 102

Army: revolts, 56-57, 60. *See also* Military governments
Art: Brazilian, *122-123,* 124-125; Indian, 121
Auto industry, 24, 68, *86-87,* 88, 90, 91, *96-97,* 102
Azevedo, Aluísio, 119
Azevedo, Fernando de: *Brazilian Culture* (book), 114

B

Back country, 24-25, 33; deprivation of, 67-68, *116,* 119, 120
Bahia (state), 24; Administrative Center exhibition palace, 124; Bom Jesus da Lapa, 117; cuisine of, *124-125;* independence movement in, 48-49; sugar industry in, 45; tobacco industry in, *89*
Bandeirantes, 46, *48,* 54
Bates, Henry Walter, 146
Bauxite mining, 22, 100
Beaches, *34-41*
Belém, 21, 139, 142
Belém-Brasília Highway, *map* 15, 90
Belo Horizonte, 26; Church of São Francisco, *123;* Fiat motor vehicle factory, *86*
Bernades, Sérgio, 124
Birth rate, 12, 66
Blumenau, 29
Boas, Claudio Villas, 148
Boca do Rio, *35*
Bom Jesus da Lapa, 117
Branco, Gerson Castelo, 124
Brasília: building of, 17, 19, 60, *61,* 123-124; Central Bank building, *96;* inauguration date, 17, 19; parliamentary offices, *16-17;* population of, 19; schools in, 70
Brazil: *maps* 15, 19; discovery of, 43; earliest chart of, *42;* naming of, 22; topographical details of, 20-21, 28-29
Brazilian Negro Front, the, 76-77
Brazilwood tree, 22, 24, *42,* 43
British merchants, 19th-century, 49
Bureaucracy, state, 96-97

C

Cabral, Admiral Pedro Álvares, 21, 43, *54*
Caeté Indians, 45
Cameron, James: quoted, 24
Caminha, Pero Vaz de, 43
Campelo, Glanco, 124
Campos Basin, 100
Candangos, 19, 20
Candomblé (cult), 117-118, 129
Capoeira, 126
Capybaras, *153*
Carajás mining complex, *98-99,* 100, 151
Cariocas, 36-37
Carvajal, Gaspar de, 137
Casaldáliga, Dom Pedro, 154
Castro Alves, Antônio de, 118, 119
Cattle industry, *8-9,* 29, *78-85;* failure in Amazonia, 148, 150
Ceará (state), *18;* Juàzeiro do Norte, 12-13; peasant women in, *25*

Cicero, Padre, *131*
CIMI, 154
Civil servants: corruption of, 60, 96; move to Brasília, 19, 60; salaries of, 65
Cladas, Zamine, 124
Class structure, 63-65, 66, 74, 76
Coconut palm, *34-35*
Coffee industry, 21, 22, 24, 26, 28, 53, *55,* 56, 88, *91*
"Color" groups, 22-23, 24, 33, 45-46, *68-69*
Commissão Pastoral de Terra (CPT), 150
Condamine, La. *See* La Condamine, Charles Marie de
Congonhas: Sanctuary of Bom Jesus, 54, 117; statue of Hosea at, *120*
Congress, Brazilian, 33, 76
Conselheiro, O (Antônio Maciel), 119-120
Construction industry, 8, 69, 91, 93, *104-105*
Copacabana Beach, *6-7, 36-37, 40-41,* 52
"Copacabana 18," the, 56
Copper mining, *98-99*
Cordel literature, *116*
Costa, Lúcio, 17, 123-124
CPT. *See* Commissão Pastoral de Terra
Crato, 130
Crime rates, 73, 93
Cuisine: African influence on, 115-116; in Bahia, 124
Cults, spiritist, 114, 115; Candomblé, 117-118, 129; Macumba, 118, 129, *132-133;* of Tia Neiva, *134-135*
Cunha, Euclides da: *Rebellion in the Backlands,* 116, 119-120

D

Dams: Itaipu, 55, 98, *104-111;* Tucurui, 98, 105, 151
Darwin, Charles, 24, 146
Delfim Netto, Antônio, 90
Discrimination. *See* Racial discrimination
Divorce, 65
Domestic servants, 65, 67
Dutch settlers, 43; expulsion of, 54
Dutra, General Eurico Gaspar, 59

E

Economy, 86-102
Educational system: schools, 70, *75;* universities, 64
Electoral system, 33
EMBRAER aircraft company, 101-102
Estado Novo (New State), 58-59
Estancias (ranches), *78*

F

Family, extended: importance of, 63, 64-65
Farming. *See* Agricultural industry
Favelas (shantytowns), 20, 28, *66-67,* 71-72, 74
FEBEM depots, 73
Feminist movement, 65-67
Fernandes, Millor, 76
Fiat, 102; Belo Horizonte motor vehicle factory, *86*
Figueiredo, President João Baptista de, 66

158

Fleming, Peter: quoted, 26
Ford, Henry, 146-147
Ford Motor Company, 86, 90, 102
France: French colonists, 43, 44-45; French influence, 49
Freyre, Gilberto: *The Masters and the Slaves* (book), 63, 76, 116
FUNAI (National Indian Foundation), 148, 151
Fur trade, *30*

G

Gama, Vasco da, 43
Gauchos, *8-9*, 29, *78-85*
Geisel, General Ernesto, 66, 92
General Motors, 86, 90, 102
Gil, Gilberto, 126
Goiás (state), 30, 47; Araguaia Indian reservation, 151
Gold mining and prospectors, 22, 24, 25, 46-48, 100; on Serra Pelada, *143-145*, 150
Gondwanaland, 138
Gorotire Indian reservation, 151, 154
Goulart, João, 60, 90
Gouvea, Andrés de: quoted, 45
Government: democratic, 60, 96-97, 98, 100; military, 53, 59-60, 90-94, 96, 97-98
Grasslands, *8-9*, 29, 78
Guanabara Bay, 44-45, 49
Guedalla, Philip: quoted, 28

H

Hammocks, *127*, 142
Horto, *20*
Humboldt, Friedrich von, 146

I

Iguaçu Falls, *27*, 30
IMF. *See* International Monetary Fund
Immigrants, 29, 49, 56, 64, 72, 74; Czech, 64; German, 29, *73;* Italian, 64; Japanese, 56, 64, *72*, 74
Inconfidência Mineira, 26, 48-49
Independence movements, 26, 48-49
Indians: Amazonian, 142, 146, 147, 148, 151, *154-155;* arts and crafts, 121, 142; conversion to Christianity, 43, *44,* 45, 115, 146; and early settlers, 43, 45, 142; hostility to pioneers, 46, *48;* influence on Heitor Villa-Lobos, 121, 122; Kadiweu, 121; Kayapo, 151, 154; Kuikuru, 121; medicinal knowledge of, 155; National Indian Foundation (FUNAI), 148, 151; Parakana, 151; parks and reservations, 151, 154; and racial prejudice, 23; romanticization of, 120-121; Service for the Protection of Indians (SPI), 147, 151; Tapirapé, 142; Tucano, 121; Tupinambá, 45; Txukarramrae, 154; Yanomamo, 142, 154
International Monetary Fund, 93, 96
Ipiranga, Cry of, *51*
Iron ore, 22, 26, *99*, 100
Isabel, princess regent, 52
Itaipu Dam, 55, 98, *104-111*

J

Jaguars, *30, 153*
Jari River, 147; project, 87, *148-149*
Jefferson, Thomas, 48
Jesuit missionaries, *44,* 45, 54, 115, 142, 146
João, Dom (later João VI, king of Portugal), 49, 54-55
João Pessoa: Hotel Tambaú in, 124
João III, king of Portugal, 44
Juàzeiro do Norte, 12-13, 131

K

Kadiweu Indians, 121
Kayapo Indians, 151, 154
Kubitschek, Juscelino, 55, 59-60, 89-90; and building of Brasília, 17, 60
Kuikuru Indians, 121

L

Labor unions, 57, 89, 90, 94
Lacerda, Carlos, 59
La Condamine, Charles Marie de, 146
Lampião (The Lantern), *58-59*
Language, 29, 33, 114
Le Corbusier (Charles-Édouard Jeanneret), 123
Lisbôa, Antônio Francisco. *See* Aleijadinho, O
Literature, *116,* 118-121
Ludwig, Daniel K., 87, 148
Lula (Luiz Inácio da Silva), 94

M

Machado de Assis, Joaquim Maria, 118-119
Maciel, Antônio. *See* Conselheiro, O
Macumba (cult), 118, 129, *132-133*
Madeira River, 127, 150
Madrid, Treaty of, 54
Maloca, 154
Manaus: as center of rubber industry, 53, 56; as duty-free port, 32, *101;* homes and offices by S. M. Porto in, 124; Opera House at, 53, 55, *94-95;* waterfront at, *57*
Manganese deposits, 22, 99
Manufacturing industries, *chart* 8, 88, 102
Maria, queen of Portugal, 49
Mato Grosso (state), *map* 15, 30, 47; Indian reservations in, 151; new towns in, *136-137*
Milhaud, Darius, 125-126
Military governments, 53, 59-60; and the economy, 53, 90-94, 96, 97-98
Minas Gerais: churches in, 116; joins Liberal Alliance, 56; Minas Conspiracy, 26, 48-49; mining in, 25-26, 46, 47
Mining industry, *chart* 8, 22, *98-99,* 100; in 17th and 18th centuries, 25-26, 46. *See also* Gold mining
Miranda, Carmen, *119*
Modernist movement, 120
Mortality rate, infant, 12, 30, 71
Mota Silva, Djanira da, 124
Mulattoes, *69,* 74, 76
Music and musicians, 55, 113-114, *118,* 121-123, 125-126

N

Napoleon Bonaparte, 49
Nascimento, Abdias do, 77
Negro, Río, *57,* 138; Tucano Indians, 121
Neiva, Tia, 134
Nepotism, 64-65
Neves, Tancredo, 96
Newspapers, 63, 76
Niemeyer, Oscar, 17, 19, 60, 123, 124
Northern Perimeter Highway, *map* 15
Novacap, 17, 19
Nuclear power program, 92, 97, 100

O

Oil industry, 22, 89, *96,* 100
Olinda, Carnival in, 113
Orellana, Francisco de, 137
Otter, giant, *152, 153*
Ouro Prêto, 25-26, *28;* churches, 116

P

Pampas, *8-9,* 29, *78-79*
Pan-American Highway, *map* 15
Pará (state), 15, 146-147; Beiradão, *147;* Tumucumaque Indian reservation, 151
Paraguay River, 21, 121
Parakana Indians, 151
Paraná (state), *21,* 29; coffee plantations in, *91*
Paraná River, 21, 29. *See also* Itaipu Dam
Parentela, 63, 64-65
Peçanha, President Nilo, 76
Pedro I, Dom, 49, *50-51*
Pedro II, Dom, 51-53
Pernambuco, 68; independence movement in, 49; sugar plantations in, 45
Petrobras, 89, 96, 100
Piauí: house by G. C. Branco at, 124.
Pinzón, Captain Vincente Yáñez, 138
Piranha, *52-53*
Plastic surgery industry, 67
Political system, 33, 53
Population, 12; "color" groups, 23; distribution, 19, 23; growth, 22
Portinari, Cândido, 123; *Café* (painting), *122;* mural of Saint Francis, *123*
Porto, Severiano Mario, 124
Pôrto Velho, *map* 15
Portuguese: colonists, 22, 43-44, 45; emigration of, 48; take over direct rule of Brazil, 49, 51
Poverty, 67-68, 71-73
Prado, Paulo: *Portrait of Brazil* (book), 121
PT. *See* Workers' party

Q

Qaratem, Nunzio, 101
Quadros, Jânio, 60, 90
Quinine, discovery of, 146

R

Racial discrimination, 23, 76-77; Unified Black Movement against Racial Discrimination, 77
Railroads, 51-52, 89, 92, 97
Recife, 21; early settlements around, 24

Religion. *See* Roman Catholic Church; Cults, spiritist
Republic, establishment of the, 52-53
Rio de Janeiro, *6-7*, 26, 28; arrival of British merchants in, 49; beaches at, 21, 26, *36-37, 40-41;* Botanical Gardens, 49; capital transferred to, 48; Carnival in, *10-11*, 28, 113, *115;* crime in, 73; establishment of, 44-45; *favelas* in, 28, *67;* first hotel in, 49; gold as foundation of wealth in, 25, 26; independence movement in, 49; Macumba cult, *132-133;* National Development Bank building, 96; National Housing Bank building, 96; Petrobras building, 96; under Prince Regent Dom João, 49; Sambódromo, *10-11;* Urca, *70*
Rio Grande do Norte: Areia Branca salt pans, *92*
Rio Grande do Sul, 29; gauchos in, *8-9;* joins Liberal Alliance, 56
Road construction, *map* 15, 30, 32-33, 89, 90, 91, 97, 98, 148
Rolim de Moura, 150
Roman Catholic Church, 114, 116, *128-129;* establishes Commissão Pastoral de Terra, 150; and family planning, 66; and Indians, 43, 150, 154; toleration of cults by, 33, 114-115, 118, *129;* as unifying factor, 33. *See also* Jesuit missionaries
Rondon, Cândido Mariano da Silva, 147
Rondônia (state): 15, 147, 150
Roosevelt, Eleanor, 27
Roosevelt, Theodore, 53, 146
Roraima (state): Yanomamo reservation, 154
Rubber industry, 24, 32, 53, 56, 88, 146-147
Rubinstein, Artur, 123

S

Salaries: civil servants', 65; doctors', 65
Salvador, *103;* beaches in, 21, *34-35, 38-39;* as capital, 24, 26, 44, 48; Carnival in, 113, *114;* Church of Our Lord of Bonfim (Nosso Senhor do Bonfim), 117-118, *129;* Convento do Carmo, *128; favela* houses in, *67;* street stalls in, *124-125*
Samba, 113-114, 125, 126; *pelo telefone,* 55, 113; schools for learning, *10-11*, 113
Santa Catarina (state), *73*
Santos, 21
São Bernardo, 68, 69, 90; Metalworkers' Union, 94
São Francisco River, 21
São Luís, 119
São Paulo, *22*, 28; antifascism demonstration in (1978), 77; auto factories in, 68, 69; *bandeirantes* in 46; coffee oligarchy in, 56; crime rate in, 72-73, 93; *favelas* in, 71, 93; foundation of, 44; gold as foundation of wealth in, 25; homeless children in, *64*, 72-73; Japanese in, *72;* migration to, 28, 68-69; population of, *23*, 28; rebellion in (1932), 57; suburbs of, 90; Week of Modern Art (1922), *55*, 120

São Vicente, 44, 45
Sarney, President José, 96, 98
Sassi, Mario, 134
Schlesinger, Arthur: quoted, 19
Schools, 70, *74-75*
Schultes, Richard, 155
Sculpture, 115, 116-117, *120*, 124
Serra Pelada: gold mine, *143-145*, 150
Sertão. See Back country
Servants, domestic, 65, 67
Service for the Protection of Indians (SPI), 147, 151
Silva, Luiz Inácio da. *See* Lula
Slave trade. *See* Afro-Brazilian blacks
Sloths: arboreal, *152-153;* three-toed, *152*
Soccer, *40-41, 112-113,* 126
Sousa, Admiral Martim Alfonso de, 43-44
Sousa, Governor General Tomé de, 44
Soybean production, 97
SPI. *See* Service for the Protection of Indians
Spiritist cults. *See* Cults, spiritist
Spix, J. B. de, 53
Steel industry, 59, 88, 89, 92, 102
SUDAM, 96, 148
SUDECO, 96
SUDENE, 96
SUDESUL, 96
Suffrage, female, 57
Sugar industry, 13, 20, 24, 25, 45, 46, 88; and distillation of alcohol, *97,* 100

T

Tapirapé Indians, 142
Tenentes, 56, 57
Timber industry, 21-22, 24, *32*, 87
Tiradentes. *See* Xavier, Joaquim José da Silva
Tobacco industry, 22, 46, *89*
Tomlinson, H. M.: quoted, 30
Tordesillas, Treaty of, 54
Trans-Amazonian Highway, *map* 15, *30-31*, 32-33, 91, 97, 98, 148
Tucano Indians, 121
Tucurui Dam, 98, 105, 151
Tumucumaque Indian reservation, 151
Tupinambá Indians, 45
Txukarramrae Indians, 154

U

Unemployment, 93
Universities, 64
Uranium deposits, 100, 154
Uruguay River, 21, 29

V

Valley of the Dawn, *134-135*
Vaqueiros, 24
Vargas, Getúlio, *55*, 56-59, 77, 88, 89
Vatapá, 124
Vieira, Father António, *44,* 146
Villa-Lobos, Heitor, 55, *118*, 121-123
Volkswagen motor vehicle company, 86, 90, 102
Volta Redonda steel mills, 59, 89

W

Wallace, Alfred Russel, 146
Water resources, 105
White Arrow, *134*
Wickham, Henry, 56
Wildlife, *52-53*, 138-139, 146, *152-153*
Women. *See* Feminist movement
Wood-pulp industry, 87, *148-149*
Workers' party (PT), 94, 96
World War I, 56
World War II, 29, 58-59, 65

X

Xavier, Joaquim José da Silva (Tiradentes), 26, 48-49
Xingu Indian reservation, 151
Xingu River: Kuikuru Indians, 121; Txukarramrae Indians, 154

Y

Yanomamo Indians, 142, 154
Yemanjá (African god), 132, 133

Z

Zweig, Stefan, 120